AF517894

CYBER CRIME

CYBER CRIME

Harish Goel

RAJAT PUBLICATIONS
NEW DELHI - 110 002 (INDIA)

RAJAT PUBLICATIONS
4740/23, Ansari Road, Daryaganj
New Delhi- 110 002 (India)
Phones : +91-11-23267924, +91-9811484973
Email: rajat_publication@yahoo.com

Cyber Crime

© *Reserved*

Edition 2026

ISBN 978-81-7880-264-0

[The responsibility for facts stated opinion expressed or conclusions reached and plagiarism, if any, in this volume is entirely that of the Editor. The publisher bears no responsibility for them whatsoever.]

PRINTED IN INDIA

Published by Mrs. Seema Wasan for **Rajat Publications**

Preface

Today computers have come a long way, with neural networks and nano-computing promising to turn every atom in a glass of water into a computer capable of performing a billion operations per second. Cyber crime is an evil having its origin in the growing dependence on computers in modern life. In a day and age when everything from microwave ovens and refrigerators to nuclear power plants is being run on computers, cyber crime has assumed rather sinister implications.

Cyber crime can involve criminal activities that are traditional in nature, such as theft, fraud, forgery, defamation and mischief, all of which are subject to the Indian Penal Code. One of the important characteristic of cybercrime is its disrespect for national boundaries. Effective law enforcement is hampered by the transnational nature of cyberspace. Mechanisms of cooperation across national borders to solve and prosecute crimes are complex and slow. Cyber criminals can defy the conventional jurisdictional realms of sovereign nations, originating an attack from almost any computer in the world, passing it across multiple national boundaries, or designing attacks that appear to be originating from foreign sources. Such techniques dramatically increase both the technical and legal complexities of investigating and prosecuting cyber crimes.

Cybercrime poses great challenges for law enforcement and for society in general. To understand why this is true, it is necessary to understand why, and how, cybercrime differs from traditional, terrestrial crime.

This book provides a comprehensive overview of cybercrime and the legal, social, and technical issues that cybercrime presents. It explores the current state of computer crime, provides specific examples of criminal activities involving computers and allows readers to look at the problem of computer crime from a more disengaging position. This work will be a valuable reference tool for computer crime investigators, law enforcement agencies, policy makers, IT professionals and general public alike.

Editor

Contents

1

Introduction to Cyber Crime

Today computers have come a long way, with neural networks and nano-computing promising to turn every atom in a glass of water into a computer capable of performing a Billion operations per second. Cyber crime is an evil having its origin in the growing dependence on computers in modern life. In a day and age when everything from microwave ovens and refrigerators to nuclear power plants is being run on computers, cyber crime has assumed rather sinister implications.

The first recorded cyber crime took place in the year 1820! That is not surprising considering the fact that the abacus, which is thought to be the earliest form of a computer, has been around since 3500 B.C. in India, Japan and China. The era of modern computers, however, began with the analytical engine of Charles Babbage. In 1820, Joseph-Marie Jacquard, a textile manufacturer in France, produced the loom. This device allowed the repetition of a series of steps in the weaving of special fabrics. This resulted in a fear amongst Jacquard's employees that their traditional employment and livelihood were being threatened. They committed acts of sabotage to discourage Jacquard from further use of the new technology. This is the first recorded cyber crime.

Major cyber crimes in the recent past include the Citibank rip off. US$10 million were fraudulently transferred out of the bank and into a bank account in Switzerland. A Russian hacker group led by Vladimir Kevin, a renowned hacker, perpetrated the attack. The group compromised the bank's security systems. Vladimir was allegedly using his office computer at AO Saturn, a computer firm in St. Petersburg, Russia, to break into Citibank computers. He was finally arrested on Heathrow airport on his way to Switzerland.

At the onset, let us satisfactorily define "cyber crime" and differentiate it from "conventional Crime". 166 Computer crime can involve criminal activities that are traditional in nature, such as theft, fraud, forgery, defamation and mischief, all of which are subject to the Indian Penal Code. The abuse of computers has also given birth to a gamut of new age crimes that are addressed by the Information Technology Act, 2000. Defining cyber crimes, as "acts that are punishable by the Information Technology Act" would be unsuitable as the Indian Penal Code also covers many cyber crimes, such as email spoofing and cyber defamation, sending threatening emails etc. A simple yet sturdy definition of cyber crime would be "unlawful acts wherein the computer is either a tool or a target or both".

A computer can be the target of crime, for example, when a person intends to steal information from, or causing damage to, a computer or computer network. This can be entirely virtual, i.e. the information only exists in digital form and the damage, while real, has no physical consequence other than the machine ceases to function. In some legal systems, intangible property cannot be stolen and the damage must be visible, e.g. as resulting from a blow from a hammer. Yet denial of service attacks for the purposes of extortion may result in significant damage both to the system and the profitability of the site targeted. A further problem is that many definitions have not kept pace with the technology. For example, where the offence requires proof of a trick or deception as the operative cause of the theft, this may require the mind of a human being to change and so do or refrain from doing something that causes the loss. Increasingly, computer systems control access to goods and services. If a criminal manipulates the system into releasing the goods or authorising the services, has there been a "trick", has there been a "deception", does the machine act because it "believes" payment to have been made, does the machine have "knowledge", does the machine "do" or "refrain from doing"" something it has been programmed to do (or not). Where human-centric terminology is used for crimes relying on natural language skills and innate gullibility, definitions have to be modified to ensure that fraudulent behaviour remains criminal no matter how it is committed (consider the definition of wire fraud).

Issues surrounding hacking, copyright theft through warez, child pornography, and paedophilia (see child grooming), have become high-profile. But this emphasis fails to consider the equally real but less spectacular issues of obscene graffiti appearing on websites and "cyberstalking" or harassment that can affect everyday life. There are also problems of privacy when confidential information is lost, say, when an e-mail is intercepted whether through illegal hacking, legitimate monitoring (increasingly common in the workplace) or when it is simply read by an unauthorised or unintended person. In R v Stanford (2006) EWCA Crim 258 the defendant was charged with the unlawful interception of e-mail communications to a public company under s1(2) Regulation of Investigatory Powers Act 2000. After his resignation as deputy chairman of the company, he was found to have intercepted e-mail to and from certain persons in that company. His defence under s1(6) was that the interceptions had been made at his request by the company's computer system administrator who was excluded from criminal liability because either he was a person who had a right to control the operation or use of the system (s1 (6) (a)) or because he had the express or implied consent of such a person to make the interception (s1(6)(b)). The Court of Appeal held that to "control" for the purposes of s1(6) meant to "authorise and forbid". An administrator only has the power physically to use and operate the system. There is no control in the management sense. The objective of s1 of the Act was to protect the privacy of e-mails. If anyone with unrestricted ability to operate and use a telecommunications system were exempt from criminal liability for intercepting communications, it would defeat the purpose of the statute.

E-mail and sms messages are seen as casual communication including many things that would never be put in a letter. But, unlike spoken communication, there is no intonation and accenting, so the message can be more easily distorted or interpreted as offensive. In England and Wales, s43 Telecommunications Act 1984 makes it an offence to use a public telecommunications network to send 'grossly offensive, threatening or obscene' material, and a 'public telecommunications network' is widely enough defined to cover Internet traffic which goes through telephone lines or other cables.

Secondly, a computer can be the tool used to plan or commit an offence such as larceny or the distribution of child pornography. The growth of international data communications and in particular the Internet has made these crimes both more common and more difficult to police. and encryption techniques, criminals may conspire or exchange data with fewer opportunities for the police to monitor and intercept. This requires modification to the standard warrants for search, telephone tapping, etc.

Thirdly, a computer can be a source of evidence. Even though the computer is not directly used for criminal purposes, it is an excellent device for record keeping, particularly given the power to encrypt the data. If this evidence can obtained and decrypted, it can be of great value to criminal investigators. Thus, specialised government agencies and units have been set up to develop the necessary expertise. See below for a link to the U.S. Department of Justice's website about e-crime and its computer forensics services.

TYPES OF CYBER CRIME

Let us examine the acts wherein the computer is a tool for an unlawful act. This kind of activity usually involves a modification of a conventional crime by using computers. Some examples are:

Hacking

Hacking may be defined as, "deliberately gaining unauthorised access to an information system" and, in extreme cases, it may amount to industrial espionage or a national security crime when the defendant accesses commercially or nationally sensitive materials. Under English law, the Computer Misuse Act 1990 creates three offences which reflect the range of seriousness in what may be done. Thus, out of curiosity or a sense of public duty, white hat hackers may identify and exploit security flaws. Although this may represent a threat to commercially or militarily sensitive sites, this form of activity is not necessarily against the public interest and should be distinguished from both nuisance attacks and the more serious, malicious assaults, even though all "victims" may still incur financial "loss" whether through the unexpected cost of having to repair insecure systems, or downtime on a retail portal. The more genuinely criminal can be external threats, i.e. those who wish to break into the systems from outside, or internal in that employees wish to steal from their employers or to place a logic bomb or similar presents when leaving their employment. The cost and inconvenience involved can be substantial.

For example, the development of computer viruses such as the "love bug", worms, trojans, etc. represent major threats. Less obvious but no less costly is telephone hacking or "phreaking", i.e. unauthorised access into an organisation's telephone system to make free long-distance calls. Even New Scotland Yard was a victim and lost £1 million when hackers accessed the DISA (Direct Inward System Access) facility on the main PBX (DISA allows teleworkers at home or travelling to call into the corporate telephone system, enter an authorisation code and gain access to system features or make long distance calls).

Hacking frequently involves people acting in different states. Criminal jurisdiction is usually invoked both when the defendant and/or the accessed computer is physically within the territory of the prosecuting state.

Internet Fraud

Internet fraud is any dishonest misrepresentation of fact intended to induce another to do or refrain from doing something which causes loss. In this context, the fraud will result in obtaining a benefit by:

- altering computer input in an unauthorised way. This requires little technical expertise and is a not uncommon form of theft by employees altering the data before entry or entering false data, or by entering unauthorised instructions or using unauthorised processes;

- altering, destroying, suppressing, or stealing output, usually to conceal unauthorised transactions: this is difficult to detect;
- altering or deleting stored data; or
- altering or misusing existing system tools or software packages, or altering or writing code for fraudulent purposes. This requires real programming skills and is not common.

Manipulating banking systems to make unauthorised electronic funds transfers or to divert the whole or part of the retail prices collected by a portal would be serious thefts. An increasing problem is the unauthorised use of credit card numbers and other data collected as part of identity theft.

Confidence tricks and scams

Despite the fact that many of these cons that trade on human gullibility are genuinely old and notorious, the internet gives criminals the opportunity to reach millions of innocent people who may be tempted by the prospect of easy money, e.g. the Nigerian banking scam.

Sale of Illegal Articles

This would include sale of narcotics, weapons and wildlife etc., by posting information on websites, auction websites, and bulletin boards or 167 simply by using email communication. E.g. many of the auction sites even in India are believed to be selling cocaine in the name of 'honey'.

Online Gambling

There are millions of websites; all hosted on servers abroad, that offer online gambling. In fact, it is believed that many of these websites are actually fronts for money laundering.

Intellectual Property Crimes

These include software piracy, copyright infringement, trademarks violations, theft of computer source code etc.Most states have enacted laws to protect copyrighted materials, and people who distribute and download copyrighted recordings without permission are liable to face civil actions for damages and penalties and/or criminal prosecution. For the most part, the criminal law is only used for commercial piracy except where a non-commercial distribution has a not-insignificant effect on the copyright owner's business. The theft of software, the copying of licensed software without permission, and software counterfeiting are not only a matter for the police but can also involve customs officers, agencies tasked to protect consumers and/or IPR holders, and agencies responsible for ensuring that advertising is not misleading.

In English law, ss16 and 20 Copyright, Designs & Patents Act 1988 (as amended by the Copyright, etc. and Trade Marks (Offences and Enforcement) Act 2002) create offences when, knowing or reasonably suspecting that the software packages, games, films, books or music files are illegal copies, and without the permission of the copyright owner, a person:

- makes unauthorised copies e.g. burning music files or films on to CD-Rs or DVD-Rs;
- distributes, sells or hires out unauthorised copies of CDs, VCDs and DVDs;

- on a larger scale, distributes unauthorised copies as a commercial enterprise on the internet;
- possesses unauthorised copies with a view to distributing, selling or hiring these to other people;
- while not dealing commercially, distributes unauthorised copies on such a scale as to have a measurable impact on the copyright owner's business.

The penalties for these "copyright theft" offences depend on the seriousness of the offences:

- before a magistrates' Court, the penalties for distributing pirated files are a maximum fine of £5,000 and/or six months imprisonment;
- in the Crown Court, the penalties for distributing pirated files are an unlimited fine and/or up to 10 years imprisonment.

Also note s24 Copyright and Related Rights Regulations 2003 which creates a range of offences relating to the distribution of any device, product or component which is primarily designed, produced, or adapted for the purpose of enabling or facilitating the circumvention of effective technological measures. When this is for non-commercial purposes, it requires there to be a measurable effect on the rights holder's business.

Pornography

A substantial quantity of both hardcore and softcore pornography, including material designed to appeal to paedophiles, is available on the Internet. Ostensibly, it is aimed at adults and it may or may not be illegal for adults to read or view depending on the rules of the state of residence. Child pornography is illegal in most states. Even if the pornography is not illegal per se, it may nevertheless be considered harmful or distressing for others to see, whether as adults coming across it unexpectedly or as children. The various offences relate to possession, storage and distribution of obscene material, although some states do not criminalise mere possession so long as there is no attempt to show it to others, and then only if distribution is for gain. But child pornography, which features the sexual abuse of children, is often considered so serious that mere possession is an offence. The general test of "obscenity" is whether the material tends to "deprave and corrupt" those who are likely to read, see, or hear it.

Offensive Content

The content of websites and other electronic communications may be harmful, distasteful or offensive for a variety of reasons. Most states have enacted law that place some limits on the freedom of speech and ban racist, blasphemous, politically subversive, seditious or inflammatory material that tends to incite hate crimes. This is a sensitive area in which the courts can become involved in arbitrating between groups with entrenched beliefs, each convinced that their point of view has been unreasonably attacked.

In England, s28 Crime and Disorder Act 1998 defines a racial group, following Mandla v Dowell-Lee (1983) 2 AC 548 (in which a requirement to wear a cap as part of a school uniform had the effect of excluding Sikh boys whose religion required them to wear a turban), as a group of persons defined by reference to race, colour, nationality (including citizenship) or ethnic or national origin; and a religious group as a group of persons defined by reference to religious belief or lack of religious belief. Therefore, it is equally an offence to show hostility to a person who practises a particular faith as to a person who has no religious belief or faith.

Harassment

Whereas content may be offensive in a non-specific way, harassment directs obscenities and derogatory comments at specific individuals focusing on gender, race, religion, nationality, sexual orientation. This often occurs in chat rooms, through newsgroups, and by sending hate e-mail to interested parties.

In England, in a broader form than s43 Telecommunications Act 1984, s1 Malicious Communications Act 1988 makes it an offence to send an indecent, offensive or threatening letter, electronic communication or other article to another person. Now, s2 Protection from Harassment Act 1997 criminalises a course of conduct amounting to harassment which the defendant knows, or ought to know, amounts to harassment of another. If a reasonable person in possession of the same information would think the course of conduct amounted to harassment of the other, the knowledge will be imputed to the defendant.

Although harassment is not defined, s7 states that it includes causing alarm or distress, and conduct is defined as including speech in all its forms. In DPP v Collins (2006) 1 WLR 308 the defendant repeatedly telephoned the offices of his MP on a wide range of political matters. In conversations with employees at the office and on messages left on the telephone answering machine, he used racist terms to show the frustration he felt at the way in which his affairs were being handled.

No-one was personally offended, but the staff became depressed. Charged under s127(1) Communications Act 2003, the magistrates found that the terms were offensive but that a reasonable person would not find them grossly offensive. To determine whether any message content is merely offensive or grossly offensive depended on their particular circumstances and context, i.e. in the wider society which is an open and just multi-racial society, the test of offensiveness was objective.

More problematic are deliberate attacks which amount to defamation although, in March 2006, Michael Keith-Smith became the first person to win damages from an individual internet user after she accused him of being a 'sex offender' and 'racist blogger' on a Yahoo! discussion site. She also claimed that his wife was a prostitute. The High Court judge decided that Tracy Williams, of Oldham, was "particularly abusive" and "her statements demonstrated that ... she had no intention of stopping her libellous and defamatory behaviour". She was ordered to pay £10,000 in damages, plus £7,200 costs. In general, libel is not treated as a criminal matter except when it may provoke the person defamed into retaliatory violence. All forms of unsolicited e-mail and advertisements can also be considered to be forms of Internet harassment where the content is offensive or of an explicit sexual nature. Now termed SPAM, it has been criminalised in various countries.

Email Spoofing

A spoofed email is one that appears to originate from one source but actually has been sent from another source. E.g. Pooja has an e-mail address pooja@asianlaws.org. Her enemy, Sameer spoofs her e-mail and sends obscene messages to all her acquaintances. Since the e-mails appear to have originated from Pooja, her friends could take offence and relationships could be spoiled for life.

Email spoofing can also cause monetary damage. In an American case, a teenager made millions of dollars by spreading false information about certain companies whose shares he had short sold. This misinformation was spread by sending spoofed emails, purportedly from news agencies like Reuters, to share brokers and investors who were informed that the companies were doing very badly. Even after the truth came out the values of the shares did not go back to the earlier levels and thousands of investors lost a lot of money.

Forgery

Counterfeit currency notes, postage and revenue stamps, mark sheets etc can be forged using sophisticated computers, printers and scanners. Outside many colleges across India, one finds touts soliciting the sale of fake mark sheets or even certificates. These are made using computers, and high quality scanners and printers. In fact, this has becoming a booming business involving thousands of Rupees being given to student gangs in exchange for these bogus but authentic looking certificates.

Cyber Defamation

This occurs when defamation takes place with the help of computers and / or the Internet. E.g. someone publishes defamatory matter about someone on a website or sends e-mails containing defamatory information to all of that person's friends. In a recent occurrence, Surekha (names of people have been changed), a young girl was about to be married to Suraj. She was really pleased because despite it being an arranged marriage, she had liked the boy. He had seemed to be open-minded and pleasant. Then, one day when she met Suraj, he looked worried and even a little upset. He was not really interested in talking to her. When asked he told her that, members of his family had been receiving e-mails that contained malicious things about Surekha's character. Some of them spoke of affairs, which she had had in the past. He told her 168 that, his parents were justifiably very upset and were also considering breaking off the engagement. Fortunately, Suraj was able to prevail upon his parents and the other elders of his house to approach the police instead of blindly believing what was contained in the mails. During investigation, it was revealed that the person sending those e-mails was none other than Surekha's stepfather. He had sent these e-mails so as to break up the marriage. The girl's marriage would have caused him to lose control of her property of which he was the guardian till she got married.

Another famous case of cyber defamation occurred in America. All friends and relatives of a lady were beset with obscene e-mail messages appearing to originate from her account. These mails were giving the lady in question a bad name among her friends. The lady was an activist against pornography. In reality, a group of people displeased with her views and angry with her for opposing them had decided to get back at her by using such underhanded methods. In addition to sending spoofed obscene e-mails they also put up websites about her, that basically maligned her character and sent e-mails to her family and friends containing matter defaming her.

Cyber Terrorism

A cyber crime is generally a domestic issue, which may have international consequences, however cyber terrorism is a global concern, which has domestic as well as international consequences. The common form of these terrorist attacks on the internet is by distributed denial of service attacks, hate websites and hate emails, attacks on sensitive computer networks, etc. Technology savvy terrorists are using 512-bit encryption, which is next to impossible to decrypt. The recent example may be cited of—Osama Bin Laden, the LTTE, attack on America's army deployment system during Iraq war. Cyber terrorism may be defined to be "the premeditated use of disruptive activities, or the threat thereof, in cyber space, with the intention to further social, ideological, religious, political or similar objectives, or to intimidate any person in furtherance of such objectives"

Another definition may be attempted to cover within its ambit every act of cyber terrorism. A terrorist means a person who indulges in wanton killing of persons or in violence or in disruption of services or means of communications essential to the community or in damaging property with the view to—

(1) putting the public or any section of the public in fear; or

(2) affecting adversely the harmony between different religious, racial, language or regional groups or castes or communities; or

(3) coercing or overawing the government established by law; or

(4) endangering the sovereignty and integrity of the nation.

A cyber terrorist is the person who uses the computer system as a means or ends to achieve the above objectives. Every act done in pursuance thereof is an act of cyber terrorism.

Cyber Criminals

The cyber criminals constitute of various groups/category. This division may be justified on the basis of the object that they have in their mind. The following are the category of cyber criminals:

1. *Children and adolescents between the age group of 6 - 18 years*: The simple reason for this type of delinquent behaviour pattern in children is seen mostly due to the inquisitiveness to know and explore the things. Other cognate reason may be to prove themselves to

be outstanding amongst other children in their group. Further the reasons may be psychological even.

2. *Organised hackers*: These kinds of hackers are mostly organised together to fulfil certain objective. The reason may be to fulfil their political bias, fundamentalism, etc. The Pakistanis are said to be one of the best quality hackers in the world. They mainly target the Indian government sites with the purpose to fulfil their political objectives.

3. *Professional hackers/crackers*: Their work is motivated by the colour of money. These kinds of hackers are mostly employed to hack the site of the rivals and get credible, reliable and valuable information. Further they are ven employed to crack the system of the employer basically as a measure to make it safer by detecting the loopholes.

4. *Discontented employees:* This group include those people who have been either sacked by their employer or are dissatisfied with their employer. To avenge they normally hack the system of their employee.

Computer criminal behaviour cuts across a wide spectrum of society, with the age of offenders ranging from 10 to 60 years and their skill level ranging from novice to professional. Computer criminals, therefore, are often otherwise average persons rather than super criminals possessing unique abilities and talents. Any person of any age with a modicum of skill, motivated by the technical challenge, by the potential for gain, notoriety or revenge, or by the promotion of ideological beliefs, is a potential computer criminal.

Organised computer criminal groups, composed of members from all over the world, are beginning to emerge. Corresponding with this increasing cooperation in criminal activity, the escalating underground use of electronic bulletin boards for clandestine criminal communication has been detected around the world. Rapidly improving telecommunication technology has added to the threat from external sources. Computer-based voice mailbox systems, for example, are being used by the computer criminal community to exchange stolen access numbers, passwords and software.

The motivations of those who would commit computer related crime are diverse, but hardly new. Computer criminals are driven by time-honoured motivations, the most obvious of which are greed, lust, power, revenge, adventure, and the desire to taste 'forbidden fruit'. The ability to make an impact on large systems may, as an act of power, be gratifying in and of itself. The desire to inflict loss or damage on another may also spring from revenge, as when a disgruntled employee shuts down an employer's computer system, or to ideology, as when one defaces the web page of an institution that one regards as abhorrent. Much activity on the electronic frontier entails an element of adventure, the exploration of the unknown. The very fact that some activities in cyberspace are likely to elicit official condemnation is sufficient to attract the defiant, the rebellious, or the irresistibly curious. Given the degree of technical competence required to commit many computer-related crimes, there is one other motivational dimension worth noting here. This, of course, is the intellectual challenge of mastering complex systems. None of the above motivations is new. The element of novelty resides in the unprecedented capacity of technology to facilitate acting on these motivations.

Cyber Crime Prevention

Almost all developed and developing countries have established rules and regulations to control and cyber crime. In India, The Information Technology Act 2000 was undoubtedly a welcome step at a time when there was no legislation on this specialised field. The Act has however during its application has proved to be inadequate to a certain extent. The hurry in which the legislation was passed, without sufficient public debate, did not really serve the desired purpose. Experts are of the opinion that one of the reasons for the inadequacy of the legislation has been the hurry in which it was passed by the parliament and it is also a fact that sufficient time was not given for public debate.

Cyber laws, in their very preamble and aim, state that they are targeted at aiding e-commerce, and are not meant to regulate cyber crime. The main intention of the legislators has been to provide for a law to regulate the e-commerce and with that aim the I.T.Act 2000 was passed, which also is one of the reasons for its inadequacy to deal with cases of cyber crime. The recent cases including Cyber stalking cyber harassment, cyber nuisance, and cyber defamation have shown that the I.T.Act 2000 has not dealt with those offences. Further it is also contended that in future new forms of cyber crime will emerge which even need to be taken care of. Therefore India should sign the cyber crime convention. However the I.T.Act 2000 read with the Penal Code is capable of dealing with these felonies.

Cyber crime in the Act is neither comprehensive nor exhaustive. We need dedicated legislation on cyber crime that can supplement the Indian Penal Code. The IT Act, 2000 is not comprehensive enough and doesn't even define the term 'cyber crime. India, as a nation, has to cope with an urgent need to regulate and punish those committing cyber crimes, but with no specific provisions to do so.

Supporters of the Indian Penal Code School vehemently argue that IPC has stood the test of time and that it is not necessary to incorporate any special laws on cyber crime. This is because it is debated by them that the IPC alone is sufficient for all kinds of crime. However, in practical terms, the argument does not have appropriate backing. It has to be distinctly understood that cyber crime and cyber space are completely new whelms, where numerous new possibilities and opportunities emerge by the day in the form of new kinds of crimes.

A new legislation on cyber crime is totally unwarranted. The reason is that the new legislation not come alone but will bring with it the same confusion, the same dissatisfaction and the same desire to supplant it by further new legislation. Mr. Duggal has stated above the need to supplement IPC by a new legislation. If that is the issue then the present legislation along with the Penal Code when read harmoniously and co-jointly is sufficient to deal with the present problems of cyber crime. Further there are other legislations to deal with the intellectual property crimes on the cyber space such as the Patents Act, Copy Right Act, Trade Marks Act. The need of the hour is a worldwide uniform cyber law to combat cyber crime. Cyber crime is a global phenomenon and therefore the initiative to fight it should come from the same level. One important reason that the Act of 2000 is not achieving complete success is the lack of awareness among the netizens about their rights. Further most of the cases are going unreported. If the people are vigilant about their rights the law definitely protects their right.

With the ever-growing arms of cyber space the territorial concept seems to vanish. New methods of dispute resolution should give way to the conventional methods. The Act of 2000 is very silent on these issues. The government has taken a leap in this direction by constituting cyber crime cells in all metropolitan and other important cities. Further the establishment of the Cyber

Crime Investigation Cell (CCIC) of the Central Bureau of Investigation (CBI) 11) is definitely a welcome step in this direction. There are many cases in which the C.B.I has achieved success.

Prevention is always better than cure. It is always better to take certain precaution while operating the net. A netizen should make them his part of cyber life. He should keep in mind the following things:

1. To prevent cyber stalking avoid disclosing any information pertaining to oneself. This is as good as disclosing your identity to strangers in public place.
2. Always avoid sending any photograph online particularly to strangers and chat friends as there have been incidents of misuse of the photographs.
3. always use latest and up date anti virus software to guard against virus attacks.
4. Always keep back up volumes so that one may not suffer data loss in case of virus contamination.
5. Never send your credit card number to any site that is not secured, .to guard against frauds.
6. Always keep a watch on the sites that your children are accessing to prevent any kind of harassment or depravation in children.
7. It is better to use a security programme that gives control over the cookies and send information back to the site as leaving the cookies unguarded might prove fatal.
8. Web site owners should watch traffic and check any irregularity on the site. Putting host-based intrusion detection devices on servers may do this.
9. Use of firewalls may be beneficial.

2

Computer Viruses and Worms

Computer Viruses

The term "virus" was first used in an academic publication by Fred Cohen in his 1984 paper *Experiments with Computer Viruses,* where he credits Len Adleman with coining it. However, a 1972 science fiction novel by David Gerrold, When H.A.R.L.I.E. Was One, includes a description of a fictional computer program called "VIRUS" that worked just like a virus and John Brunner's 1975 novel The Shockwave Rider describes programs known as "tapeworms" which spread through a network for deleting data. The term "computer virus" with current usage also appears in the comic book "Uncanny X-Men" No. 158, published in 1982. Therefore, Although Cohen's use of "virus" may, perhaps, have been the first "academic" use, the term had been used earlier.

Viruses have been around almost as long as computers themselves, and they account for untold billions of dollars of damage every year. While there are many different types of viruses, the best protection against them is to exhibit extreme caution when downloading files from the internet and opening e-mail attachments and to religiously avail yourself of one of the many antivirus software programs currently on the market. Computer viruses may be benign and result only in amusement or slight annoyance. The best known example of such a virus are some versions of the 'Stoned' virus which simply write "Your computer is stoned" on the monitor. Other viruses are more malignant and malicious, destroying or altering data. Once a virus is active in a host computer, the infection can spread rapidly throughout a network to other systems. A virus may attach itself to other programs and hide in them. Or it may infiltrate the computer's operating system. All computer operating systems, are vulnerable, some more than others.

Viruses enter computer systems from an external software source. Just as flowers are attractive to the bees that pollinate them, virus host programs are deliberately made attractive to victims. Often the attraction will be a new game made available for downloading from a computer bulletin board. Or it may be disguised as an executable file attached to an electronic mail message from a friend or business associate. Springing up seemingly from nowhere, spreading like wildfire, computer viruses attack computer systems large and small, damaging files and rendering computers and networks unusable. They proliferate through e-mail, internet file downloads, and shared diskettes.

The points where your computer is vulnerable to viruses are:

- *Floppy disks and CDs*: Floppy disks can have a virus in the boot sector. They can also hold infected programs or documents. CDs may also hold infected items.
- *Programs*: Programs that carry a virus can infect your machine as soon as you run them.
- *Documents and spreadsheets*: These can contain macro viruses, which can infect and make changes to other documents or spreadsheets.

- *The internet*: Downloaded programs or documents may be infected.
- *Email*: Email can include infected attachments. If you double-click on an infected attachment, you risk infecting your machine. Some emails even include malicious scripts that run as soon as you preview the mail or read the body text.

Tens of millions of computers are infected by computer viruses every year. In 2001, 2.3 million computers were infected by the SirCam virus, and another million computers were hit by CodeRed. Even worse, the LoveLetter virus hit an estimated 45 million computers-on a single day in 2000. ICSA Labs, a leading provider of security research, intelligence, and certification, found that the rate of virus infection in North America in 2001 was 113 infections per 1000 computers-meaning that more than 10% of all computers they surveyed had been hit by a virus. And this rate is increasing; ICSA says that the likelihood of contracting a computer virus has doubled for each of the past five years. Viruses hit the corporate world especially hard; a single infected computer can spread the virus among the entire corporate network. McAfee.com, a company specialising in virus protection, estimates that two-third of U.S. companies are attacked by viruses each year. A third of those companies reported that viruses knocked out their servers for an average of 5.8 hours per infection, and 46% of the companies required more than 19 days to completely recover from the virus incident.

Functioning of Computer Virus

A computer virus is like a biological virus in that it also isn't an independent entity; it must piggyback on a host in order to propagate. Many viruses are hidden in the code of legitimate software programs-programs that have been "infected," that is. These viruses are called file infector viruses, and when the host program is launched, the code for the virus is also executed, and the virus loads itself into your computer's memory. From there, the virus code searches for other programs on your system that it can infect; if it finds one, it adds its code to the new program, which, now infected, can be used to infect other computers.

If all a virus did was copy itself to additional programs and computers, there would be little harm done, save for having all our programs get slightly larger. Unfortunately, most viruses not only replicate themselves, they also perform other operations-many of which are wholly destructive. A virus might, for example, delete certain files on your computer. It might overwrite the boot sector of your hard disk, making the disk inaccessible. It might write messages on your screen, or cause your system to emit rude noises. It might also hijack your e-mail program and use the program to send itself to all your friends and colleagues, thus replicating itself to a large number of PCs.

Viruses that replicate themselves via e-mail or over a computer network cause the subsidiary problem of increasing the amount of internet and network traffic. These fast-replicating viruses-called worms-can completely overload a company network, shutting down servers and forcing tens of thousands of users offline. While no individual machines might be damaged, this type of communications disruption can be quite costly. Most viruses are designed to deliver their payload when they're first executed. However, some viruses won't attack until specifically prompted, typically on a predetermined date or day of the week. They stay on your system, hidden from sight like a sleeper agent in a spy novel, until they're awoken on a specific date; then they go about the work they were programmed to do. In short, viruses are nasty little bits of computer code, designed to inflict as much damage as possible, and to spread to as many computers as possible-a particularly vicious combination.

Categories of computer Viruses

A computer virus is a piece of software that surreptitiously attaches itself to other programs and then does something unexpected. There are other types of programs-such as Trojan horses and worms-that do similar damage but don't embed themselves within other program code. These programs aren't technically viruses, but they pose the same danger to computer systems everywhere. For that reason, all these programs-virus and non-virus, alike-are typically lumped together and referred to, in common parlance, as viruses. Some viruses-called hybrid viruses-include aspects of more than one virus type. Sometimes it is difficult to precisely classify a computer virus and, in fact, many viruses fall into more than one category.

File Infector Viruses

The file infector virus are the most traditional form of computer virus. It hides within the code of another program. The infected program can be a business application, a utility, or even a game-just as long as it's an executable program, typically with an EXE, COM, SYS, BAT, or PIF extension. When an infected program is launched, the virus code copies itself into your computer's memory, typically before the program code is loaded. By loading itself into memory separately from the host program, the virus can continue to run in your system's memory, even after the host program is closed down. Before the advent of the internet and coincident creation of macro viruses, file infector viruses accounted for probably 85% of all virus infections. Today that number is much lower, because the other types of viruses are much easier to propagate.

Boot Sector Viruses

Boot sector viruses reside in the part of the disk that is read into memory and executed when your computer first boots up. Once loaded, the virus can then infect any other disk used by the computer; a disk-based boot sector virus can also infect a PC's hard disk. Most boot sector viruses were spread by floppy disk, especially in the days before hard disks were common. Since removable disks are less widely used today, boot sector viruses have become much less prevalent than they were in the early 1990s.

Macro Viruses

Macros are small programs that are created to do highly specific tasks within an application and are written in a pseudo-programming language designed to work with the application. The most common macro language, used in all Microsoft applications, is called Visual Basic for Applications (VBA). VBA code can be added to a Word document to create custom menus and perform automatic operations; unfortunately, VBA code can also be used to modify files and send unwanted e-mail messages, which is where the virus writers come in.

What makes macro viruses potentially more dangerous than file infector or boot sector viruses is that macros-and thus macro viruses-can be attached to document files. Older virus types had to be embedded in executable programs, which made them relatively easy to find and stop. But when any Word or Excel document you open could contain a macro virus, the world is suddenly a much more dangerous place. The widespread, relatively nonchalant sharing of data files has contributed to the huge rise in macro virus attacks. Even users who are extra-vigilant about the programs they download often don't think twice about opening a Word or Excel document they receive from another user. Because data files are shared so freely, macro viruses are able to spread rapidly from one machine to another-and run, automatically, whenever the infected document is opened.

Script Viruses

Script viruses are based on common scripting languages, which are macro-like pseudo-programming languages typically used on web sites and in some computer applications. These viruses are written into JavaScript, ActiveX, and Java applets, which often run automatically when you visit a web page or open a Word or Excel application. With the increasing use of the web, these script viruses are becoming more common-and more deadly.

Trojan Horses

A Trojan horse is a program that claims to do one thing but then does something totally different. A typical Trojan horse has a filename that makes you think it's a harmless type of file; it looks innocuous enough to be safe to open. But when you run the file, it's actually a virus program that proceeds to inflict its damage on your system. It delivers its payload through deception, just like the fabled Trojan horse of yore. Trojan horses are becoming more common, primarily through the spread of internet-based e-mail. These e-mail Trojans spread as innocent-looking attachments to e-mail messages; when you click to open the attachment, you launch the virus.

E-Mail Viruses

An e-mail virus is a program that is distributed as an attachment to an e-mail message. These viruses are typically separate programs that do their damage when they're manually executed by you, the user. These viruses masquerade as pictures, Word files, and other common attachments, but are really EXE, VBS, PIF, and other types of executable files in disguise. Many e-mail viruses hijack your e-mail program and send themselves out to all the contacts in your address book. Because of the proliferation of the internet, e-mail is the fastest-growing medium for virus delivery today.

Email is now the biggest source of viruses. As long as viruses were transferred by floppy disk, they spread slowly. Companies could ban disks or insist on having them viruschecked. Email has changed all that. Now you can exchange files much more quickly and infecting your PC is as easy as clicking on an icon or easier. Conventional viruses can spread faster and new kinds of virus exploit the workings of email programs. Some users think they are always safe to open email as long as they don't look at attachments. This is no longer necessarily true. Viruses such as Kakworm and Bubbleboy can infect users when they read email. They look like any other message but contain a hidden script that runs as soon as you open the email, or even look at it in the preview pane. This script can change system settings and send the virus to other users via email. Microsoft have issued a patch that eliminates this security weakness.

Email is a popular medium for hoaxes. These are bogus virus reports that urge you to forward the message to everyone you know. An email hoax can spread across networks like a virus and can cause a mail overload. The difference is that the hoax doesn't need virus code; it simply depends on users' credulity. The most successful viruses today are those that themselves automatically by email. Typically, these viruses depend on the user clicking on an attached document. This runs a script that uses the email program to forward infected documents to other email users. Melissa, for example, sends a message to the first fifty addresses in all address books that Microsoft Outlook can access. Other viruses send themselves to every address in the address book. The greatest security risk at present isn't email itself but email attachments. Any program, document or spreadsheet that you receive by email could carry a virus; launching such an attachment can infect your computer. Unfortunately, email attachments are a popular way to exchange information. Many users think it's 'harmless fun' to circulate screensavers, greetings cards, animations or joke programs. However, such files can carry viruses.

Even an attachment that appears to be a safe type of file, e.g. a file with a .txt extension, can pose a threat. That 'text file' may actually be a malicious VBS script with the file extension (.vbs) hidden from view. The VBS/Monopoly worm is an example of a malicious program disguised as entertainment. It masquerades as a 'Bill Gates joke'. It is (it displays a Monopoly board with Microsoft images in it) but it also emails itself to other users and forwards your system details to specific email addresses, threatening the confidentiality of sensitive information.

Internet Viruses

The internet has made more information available to more people more quickly than ever before. The downside is that the internet has also made it easier for harmful computer code to reach office and home computers. The internet has increased the risk of infection. Ten years ago, most viruses spread via floppy disks. Spreading in this way was slow and depended on users making a conscious effort to run new programs. If the virus had side-effects that were too obvious, it was unlikely to affect many users. Now that the internet is so widely used, everything has changed. Sharing software over the net is easy. A click of the mouse attaches a program to an email and it's easy to detach and run it. Users can just as easily place a program on a web page, which anyone can download. So file (or 'parasitic') viruses, which target programs, can thrive on the net.

The viruses that really benefit, though, are macro viruses, which affect documents. Users frequently download documents or spreadsheets, or exchange them by email. All you have to do to infect your computer is to click on a downloaded file or email attachment. When you use the internet, open documents with a viewer that ignores macros, and don't run programs that don't come from a trustworthy source. Visiting a website is less hazardous than opening unknown programs or documents. There are risks, though. The threat depends on the types of code used in the site and the security measures taken by service providers and by you. Here are the main types of code you will encounter.

HTML: Web pages are written in HTML (Hypertext Markup Language). This language lets web authors format their text and create links to graphics and to other pages. HTML code itself can't carry a virus. However, web pages can contain code that launches applications or opens documents automatically. This introduces the risk of launching an infected item.

ActiveX: ActiveX is a Microsoft technology for web developers used only on computers running Windows. ActiveX applets, used to create visual effects on webpages, have full access to resources on your computer, which makes them a potential threat. However, digital signatures, which prove that an applet is authentic and hasn't been tampered with, do provide limited security.

Java: People sometimes worry unduly about Java viruses on the internet. They do so because they confuse Java applets, which are used to create effects on web pages, with Java applications and Java scripts. Applets are generally safe. They are run by the browser in a secure environment known as a 'sandbox'. Even if a security flaw lets an applet escape, a malicious applet cannot spread easily. Applets usually flow from a server to users' computers, not from one user to another. In addition, applets are not saved on the hard disk, except in the web cache. If you do encounter a harmful applet, it is most likely to be a Trojan, i.e. a malicious program pretending to be legitimate software.

VBS script: BS (Visual Basic Script) can run as soon as a page is viewed, depending on the browser used. You don't have to do anything to launch it. This script is used by email worms such as Kakworm and Bubbleboy, but can just as well be run from web pages.

Backdoor Trojans: A backdoor Trojan is a program that allows someone to take control of another user's PC via the internet. Like other Trojans, a backdoor Trojan poses as legitimate or desirable software. When it is run usually on a Windows 95/98 PC), it adds itself to the PC's startup routine. The Trojan can then monitor the PC until it makes a connection to the internet. Once the PC is on-line, the person who sent the Trojan can use software on their computer to open and close programs on the infected computer, modify files and even send items to the printer. Subseven and BackOrifice are among the best known backdoor Trojans.

Instant Messaging Viruses

Many computer users like to chat online, either in public chat rooms or in private instant messaging (IM) conversations. Most chat and IM programs let you send files across to other users, and it's that capability that has contributed to the spread of so-called "instant" viruses. Just as many users are in the habit of automatically opening all attachments to their incoming e-mail messages, many users are also accustomed to accepting any files sent to them when they're chatting. Unfortunately, a significant percentage of files sent via chat or IM are virus files, often Trojan horses masquerading as photographs or helpful utilities. Downloading and then opening one of these files begins the infection process.

Cookie Viruses

Cookies do not pose a direct threat to your computer or the data on it. However, they do theaten your confidentiality: a cookie enables a website to remember your details and keep track of your visits to the site. If you prefer to remain anonymous, you should use the security settings on your browser to disable cookies. Attacks on web servers End-users aren't the only ones at risk on the internet. Some hackers target the web servers which make websites available. A common form of attack involves sending so many requests to a web server that it slows down or crashes. When this happens, genuine users can no longer gain access to the websites hosted by the server. CGI (Common Gateway Interface) scripts are another weak point. These scripts run on web servers to handle search engines, accept input from forms, and so forth. Hackers can exploit poorly-implemented CGI scripts to take control of a server. If you want to use the internet safely, you should do the following:

– *Have a separate network for internet machines:* Maintain separate networks for those computers that are connected to the internet and those that are not. Doing so reduces the risk that users will download infected files and spread viruses on your main network.

– *Use firewalls and/or routers*: A firewall admits only authorised traffic to your organisation. A router controls the flow of packets of information from the internet.

– *Configure your internet browser for security*: Disable Java or ActiveX applets, cookies, etc., or ask to be warned that such code is running.

Mobile Phone Viruses

The last decade brought the world wide web to your desktop; the next will bring it to your mobile phone. You can already access internet-like sites and services on the new generation mobiles and the technology is developing fast. But as it becomes easier to transfer data—even on the move—the risk is that new security threats will emerge too. There have been viruses that send messages to phones. For example, VBS/Timo-A, a worm that spreads itself by email, also uses the modem to send text (SMS) messages to selected mobile numbers. The notorious Love Bug virus is also capable of forwarding text to fax machines and mobiles. However, these viruses can't infect or harm the mobile phone. Things might change as mobile phones become more sophisticated.

As mobile devices become more complex, they could also become vulnerable to viruses or to hackers. The most talked-about new technology in this field is WAP (Wireless Application Protocol). WAP provides internet-type information and services for mobile phones and organisers. It is based on the same model as web communications, i.e. a central server delivers code that is run by a browser on your phone. So, at the moment, the possibilities for viruses are very limited. A virus could infect the server itself, but the chances for it to spread or to have an effect on users would be minimal. First, there is nowhere on a WAP system that a virus can copy itself or survive. Unlike a PC, a WAP phone does not store applications. The phone downloads the code it needs and keeps no copy, except temporarily in the browser cache. Second, a virus cannot yet spread from one user to another because there is no communication between client phones. In theory, a 'virus' could distribute links to malicious WAP sites, tempting users to use harmful applications, but that still involves running code from the server.

WAP uses a version of HTTP, the protocol for web pages, which could transmit more complex content than that processed by WAP browsers at present. A future generation of browsers might be able to download files, such as documents, that contain macro viruses. Under WAP, the server will soon be able to push content to mobile phones. As well as alerting users to updated information or new email, 'push' technology could download the data to the cache—without the need for you to take any action. Malicious code could exploit this system to distribute itself.

Palmtops Viruses

Palmtops or PDAs run specially written or scaled-down operating systems – such as EPOC, PalmOS and PocketPC. Such systems will eventually be able to use versions of popular desktop applications, making them vulnerable to malicious code in the same way as desktop machines. In early 2001, there were already viruses that affect the Palm system. Palmtops are also regularly connected to home or office PCs to synchronise the data on the two machines. Such data synchronisation could allow viruses to spread easily. No-one yet knows which will be more successful in the future: mobile computers or smart mobile phones. Whichever it is, the security risks will increase as mobile computers become better at communicating.

Virus Writer

A virus writer is a person with a certain amount of technical expertise. But instead of using that expertise productively, virus writers use it to generate indiscriminate mayhem among other computer users. This havoc-wreaking is, in almost all instances, deliberate. Virus writers intend to be destructive. They get some sort of kick out of causing as much damage as possible, from the relative anonymity of their computer keyboards. In addition, some developers create viruses to prove their technical prowess. Among certain developers, writing a "successful" virus provides a kind of bragging right, and demonstrates, in some warped fashion, that the writer is especially skilled.

Virus programs can be enormously destructive, and it takes a peculiar lack of ethics to deliberately perpetrate such destruction on such a wide scale. In the end, a virus writer is no better than a common vandal. Except for the technical expertise required, the difference between throwing a rock through a window and destroying PC files via a virus is minimal. Some people find pleasure in destruction, and in our high-tech age, such pleasure can come from writing destructive virus code. Unlike biological viruses, computer viruses do not simply evolve by themselves, except in the cases where copying errors and recombination have led to actual evolution of computer viruses [citation needed]; however, these cases are very rare compared to the rapid generation of new malware by human programmers. They cannot come into existence spontaneously, nor can they be created by bugs in regular programs. They are deliberately created by programmers, or by people who use virus creation software.

Virus writers can have various reasons for creating and spreading malware. Viruses have been written as research projects, pranks, vandalism, to attack the products of specific companies, to distribute political messages, and financial gain from identity theft or spyware. Some virus writers consider their creations to be works of art, and see virus writing as a creative hobby. Additionally, many virus writers oppose deliberately destructive payload routines.

Some viruses were intended as "good viruses". They spread improvements to the programs they infect, or delete other viruses. These viruses are, however, quite rare, still consume system resources, may accidentally damage systems they infect, and, on occasion, have become infected and acted as vectors for malicious viruses. Moreover, they normally operate without asking for permission of the owner of the computer. Since self-replicating code causes many complications, it is questionable if a well-intentioned virus can ever solve a problem in a way which is superior to a regular program that does not replicate itself.

Replication of Viruses

In order to replicate itself, a virus must be permitted to execute code and write to memory. For this reason, many viruses attach themselves to executable files that may be part of legitimate programs. If a user tries to start an infected program, the virus' code may be executed first. Viruses can be divided into two types, on the basis of their behaviour when they get executed. Nonresident viruses immediately search for other hosts that can be infected, infect these targets, and finally transfer control to the application program they infected. Resident viruses do not search for hosts when they are started. Instead, a resident virus loads itself into memory on execution and transfers control to the host program. The virus stays active in the background and infects new hosts when those files are accessed by other programs or the operating system itself.

Nonresident viruses can be thought of as consisting of a finder module and a replication module. The finder module is responsible for finding new files to infect. For each new executable file the finder module encounters, it calls the replication module to infect that file. For simple viruses the replicator's task is to:

- Open the new file
- Check if the executable file has already been infected
- Append the virus code to the executable file
- Save the executable's starting point
- Change the executable's starting point so that it points to the start location of the newly copied virus code
- Save the old start location to the virus in a way so that the virus branches to that location right after its execution.
- Save the changes to the executable file
- Close the infected file
- Return to the finder so that it can find new files for the replicator to infect.

Resident viruses contain a replication module that is similar to the one that is employed by nonresident viruses. However, this module is not called by a finder module. Instead, the virus loads the replication module into memory when it is executed and ensures that this module is executed each time the operating system is called to perform a certain operation. For example, the replication module can get called each time the operating system executes a file. In this case, the virus infects every suitable program that is executed on the computer. Resident viruses are sometimes subdivided into a category of fast infectors and a category of slow infectors. Fast infectors are designed to infect as many files as possible. For instance, a fast infector can infect every potential host file that is accessed. This poses a special problem to anti-virus software, since a virus scanner will access every potential host file on a computer when it performs a system-wide scan. If the virus scanner fails to notice that such a virus is present in memory, the virus can "piggy-back" on the virus scanner and in this way infect all files that are scanned.

Hosts

Viruses have targeted various types of hosts. This is a non-exhaustive list:

- Binary executable files (such as COM-files and EXE-files in MS-DOS, Portable Executable files in Microsoft Windows, and ELF files in Linux)
- Boot sectors of floppy disks and hard disk partitions
- The master boot record of a harddisk
- General-purpose script files (such as batch files in MS-DOS and Microsoft Windows, VBScript files, and shell script files on Unix-like platforms).
- Application-specific script files (such as Telix-scripts)
- Documents that can contain macros (such as Microsoft Word documents, Microsoft Excel spreadsheets, AmiPro documents, and Microsoft Access database files)

In order to avoid detection by users, some viruses employ different kinds of deception. Some old viruses, especially on the MS-DOS platform, make sure that the "last modified" date of a host file stays the same when the file is infected by the virus. This approach does not fool anti-virus software, however. Some viruses can infect files without increasing their sizes or damaging the files. They accomplish this by overwriting unused areas of executable files. These are called cavity viruses. For example the CIH virus, or Chernobyl Virus, infects Portable Executable files. Because those files had many empty gaps, the virus, which was 1 KB in length, did not add to the size of the file.

Recent viruses avoid any kind of detection attempt by attempting to forcefully kill the tasks associated with the virus scanner before it can detect them. As computers and operating systems grow larger and more complex, old hiding techniques need to be updated or replaced.

A virus needs to infect hosts in order to spread further. In some cases, it might be a bad idea to infect a host program. For example, many anti-virus programs perform an integrity check of their own code. Infecting such programs will therefore increase the likelihood that the virus is detected. For this reason, some viruses are programmed not to infect programs that are known to be part of anti-virus software. Another type of hosts that viruses sometimes avoid is bait files. Bait files (or goat files) are files that are specially created by anti-virus software, or by anti-virus professionals themselves, to be infected by a virus. These files can be created for various reasons, all of which are related to the detection of the virus:

- Anti-virus professionals can use bait files to take a sample of a virus. It is more practical to store and exchange a small infected bait file, than to exchange a large application program that has been infected by the virus.
- Anti-virus professionals can use bait files to study the behaviour of a virus and evaluate detection methods. This is especially useful when the virus is polymorphic. In this case, the virus can be made to infect a large number of bait files. The infected files can be used to test whether a virus scanner detects all versions of the virus.

– Some anti-virus software employs bait files that are accessed regularly. When these files are modified, the anti-virus software warns the user that a virus is probably active on the system.

Since bait files are used to detect the virus, or to make detection possible, a virus can benefit from not infecting them. Viruses typically do this by avoiding suspicious programs, such as small program files or programs that contain certain patterns of 'garbage instructions'. A related strategy to make baiting difficult is sparse infection. Sometimes, sparse infectors do not infect a host file that would be a suitable candidate for infection in other circumstances. For example, a virus can decide on a random basis whether to infect a file or not, or a virus can only infect host files on particular days of the week.

Some viruses try to trick anti-virus software by intercepting its requests to the operating system. A virus can hide itself by intercepting the anti-virus software's request to read the file and passing the request to the virus, instead of the OS. The virus can then return an uninfected version of the file to the anti-virus software, so that it seems that the file is "clean". Modern anti-virus software employs various techniques to counter stealth mechanisms of viruses. The only completely reliable method to avoid stealth is to boot from a medium that is known to be clean.

Most modern antivirus programs try to find virus-patterns inside ordinary programs by scanning them for so-called virus signatures. A signature is a characteristic byte-pattern that is part of a certain virus or family of viruses. If a virus scanner finds such a pattern in a file, it notifies the user that the file is infected. The user can then delete, or "clean" or "heal" the infected file. Some viruses employ techniques that make detection by means of signatures difficult or impossible. These viruses modify their code on each infection. That is, each infected file contains a different variant of the virus.

Anti-virus Software

Many users install anti-virus software that can detect and eliminate known viruses after the computer downloads or runs the executable. They work by examining the contents of the computer's memory and the files stored on fixed or removable drives, and comparing those files against a database of known virus "signatures". Some anti-virus programs are able to scan opened files in addition to sent and received emails 'on the fly' in a similar manner. This practice is known as "on-access scanning." Anti-virus software does not change the underlying capability of host software to transmit viruses. There have been attempts to do this but adoption of such anti-virus solutions can void the warranty for the host software. Users must therefore update their software regularly to patch security holes. Anti-virus software also needs to be regularly updated in order to gain knowledge about the latest threats and hoaxes.

Anti-virus software can detect viruses, prevent access to infected files and often eliminate the infection. Properties of different kinds of anti-virus software are given below.

1. *Scanners*: Virus scanners can detect, and often disinfect, the viruses known at the time the scanner is released. Scanners are easily the most popular form of anti-virus software but they have to be updated regularly to recognise new viruses. There are on-demand and on-access scanners. Many anti-virus packages offer both. On-demand scanners let you start or schedule a scan of specific files or drives. On-access scanners stay active on your machine whenever you are using it.

2. *Checksummers:* Checksummers are programs that can tell when files have been changed. If a virus infects a program or document, changing it in the process, the checksummer should report the change. The good thing about checksummers is that they do not need to know anything about a virus in order to detect its presence. For that reason, checksummers do not need regular updating. The bad thing about checksummers is that they cannot tell the difference between a virus and a legitimate change, so false alarms are likely. Checksummers have particular problems with documents, which can change frequently. In addition, checksummers can only alert you after infection has taken place, they cannot identify the virus, and they cannot provide disinfection.

3. *Heuristics*: Heuristic software tries to detect viruses— both known and unknown – by using general rules about what viruses look like. Unlike conventional scanners, this software doesn't rely on frequent updates about all known viruses. However, if a new kind of virus emerges, the software will not recognise it and will need to be updated or replaced. Heuristics can be prone to false alarms.

Computer Worms

The main difference between a computer virus and a worm is that a virus cannot propagate by itself whereas worms can. A worm uses a network to send copies of itself to other systems and it does so without any intervention. In general, worms harm the network and consume bandwidth, whereas viruses infect or corrupt files on a targeted computer. Viruses generally do not affect network performance, as their malicious activities are mostly confined within the target computer itself. The name 'worm' was taken from The Shockwave Rider, a 1970s science fiction novel by John Brunner. Researchers writing an early paper on experiments in distributed computing noted the similarities between their software and the program described by Brunner and adopted the name.

The first implementation of a worm was by two researchers at Xerox PARC in 1978. The authors, John Shoch and Jon Hupp, originally designed the worm to find idle processors on the network and assign them tasks, sharing the processing and so improving the whole network efficiency. The first worm to attract wide attention, the Morris worm, was written by Robert Tappan Morris, who at the time was a graduate student at Cornell University. It was released on November 2, 1988, and quickly infected a great number of computers on the internet at the time. It propagated through a number of bugs in BSD Unix and its derivatives. Morris himself was convicted under the US Computer Crime and Abuse Act and received three years probation, 400 hours community service and a fine in excess of $10,000. In addition to replication, a worm may be designed to do any number of things, such as delete files on a host system or send documents via e-mail. More recent worms may be multi-headed and carry other executables as a payload. However, even in the absence of such a payload, a worm can wreak havoc just with the network traffic generated by its reproduction. Mydoom, for example, caused a noticeable worldwide internet slowdown at the peak of its spread.

A common payload is for a worm to install a backdoor in the infected computer, as was done by Sobig and Mydoom. These zombie computers are used by spam senders for sending junk email or to cloak their website's address. Spammers are thought to pay for the creation of such worms, and worm writers have been caught selling lists of IP addresses of infected machines. Others try to blackmail companies with threatened DoS attacks. The backdoors can also be exploited by other worms, such as Doomjuice, which spreads using the backdoor opened by Mydoom. Whether worms can be useful is a common theoretical question in computer science and artificial intelligence. The Nachi family of worms, for example, tried to download then install patches from Microsoft's website to fix various vulnerabilities in the host system. This eventually made the systems affected more secure, but generated considerable network traffic, rebooted the machine in the course of patching it, and, maybe most importantly, did its work without the explicit consent of the computer's owner or user. As such, most security experts deprecate worms, whatever their payload.

Computer worms primarily replicate on networks, but they represent a subclass of computer viruses. Interestingly enough, even in security research communities, many people imply that computer worms are dramatically different from computer viruses. In fact, even within CARO (Computer Antivirus Researchers Organisation), researchers do not share a common view about what exactly can be classified as a "worm." We wish to share a common view, but well, at least a few of us agree that all computer worms are ultimately viruses. The network-oriented infection strategy is indeed a primary difference between viruses and computer worms. Moreover, worms usually do not need to infect files but propagate as standalone programs. Additionally, several worms can take control of remote systems without any help from the users, usually exploiting a vulnerability or set of vulnerabilities. These usual characteristics of computer worms, however, do not always hold.

Components of Computer Worms

Each computer worm has a few essential components, such as the target locator and the infection propagator modules, and a couple of other nonessential modules, such as remote control, update interface, life-cycle manager, and payload routines.

1. *Target Locator*: To spread rapidly on the network, the worm needs to be able to find new targets. Most worms search your system to discover e-mail addresses and simply send copies of themselves to such addresses. This is convenient for attackers because corporations typically need to allow e-mail messages across the corporate firewalls, thereby allowing an easy penetration point for the worm. Many worms deploy techniques to scan the network for nodes on the IP level and even "fingerprint" the remote system to check whether such a system might be vulnerable.

2. *Infection Propagator*: A very important component of the worm is the strategy the worm uses to transfer itself to a new node and get control on the remote system. Most worms assume that you have a certain kind of system, such as a Windows machine, and send you a worm compatible with such systems. For example, the author of the worm can use any script language, document format, and binary or in-memory injected code to attack your system. Typically, the attacker tricks the recipient into executing the worm based on social engineering techniques.

3. *Remote Control and Update Interface*: Another important component of a worm is remote control using a communication module. Without such a module, the worm's author cannot control the worm network by sending control messages to the worm copies. Such remote control can allow the attacker to use the worm as a DDoS (distributed denial of service) tool on the zombie network against several unknown targets.

3. *Life-Cycle Manager*: Some worm writers prefer to run a version of a computer worm for a preset period of time. For instance, the W32/Welchia.A worm "committed suicide" in early 2004, and then the B variant of Welchia was released in late February of 2004 to run for three more months. On the other hand, many worms have bugs in their life-cycle manager component and continue to run without ever stopping. Furthermore, we often encounter variants of computer worms that were patched by others to give the worm "endless" life.

4. *Payload:* Another optional but common component of a computer worm is the payload (activation routine). In many cases, computer worms do not contain any payload. An increasingly popular payload is a DoS attack against a particular Web site. However, a common side effect of computer worms is accidental DoS attacks as a result of overloaded networks, especially overloaded network routers. However, other interesting side effects have also been observed, such as accidental attacks on network printers.

5. Self-*Tracking*: Many computer virus authors are interested in seeing how many machines the virus can infect. Alternatively, they want to allow others to track the path of the virus infections. Several viruses, such as W97M/Groov.A, upload the IP information of the infected system to an FTP site. Computer worms typically send the attacker an e-mail message with information about the infected computer to track their spread. The Morris worm deployed a self-tracking module that attempted to send a UDP datagram to the host at ernie.berkeley.edu after approximately every 15 infections, but this routine was bogus, and it never sent any information.

Functions of Target Locator

An efficient target locator module is an extremely important component of computer worms. The easiest mechanism for the attacker is to collect e-mail addresses on the system on which the worm was executed and to send attachments to such targets, but there are many more sophisticated techniques to reach new targets quickly, such as random construction of IP addresses in combination with port scanning. Modern computer worms also attack the network using several protocols.

E-mail Address Collection

There are many ways in which a computer worm can collect e-mail addresses for attacks. The attacker can enumerate various address books with standard APIs, including COM interfaces. An example of this is W32/ Serot Files can be enumerated directly to find e-mail addresses within them. Additionally, sophisticated worms might use the NNTP (network news transfer protocol) to read newsgroups or use search engines such as Google to collect e-mail addresses using techniques similar to those that spam attackers use.

All computer environments have some form of address book to store contact information. For example, the Windows Address Book or the Outlook Address Book might contain the e-mail addresses of your friends, colleagues, and clients, or names of e-mail lists in which you participate. If a worm can query the e-mail addresses stored in such locations, it can send itself to all of them and spread with an exponential infection rate. Unfortunately, it is a rather trivial task to query the information in such address books. The W97M/ Melissa@mm worm was especially successful with this technique in March 1999. The worm depends on the

Microsoft Outlook installation on the system to propagate itself in e-mail by sending an infected Word document as an attachment.

Several computer worms such as W32/Magistr simply search for the e-mail client's files or for all files with a WAB extension and parse such files directly for e-mail addresses. This technique became popular after Microsoft introduced security features in Outlook against computer worms that spread via e-mail messages. As you might expect, file parsing-based attacks have their own minor caveats. For example, some worms have file format dependencies. The Windows Address Book is not saved in the same format on all Windows versions. Unicode is not always supported, and the file format is different in this case. This is why such worms cannot spread to other systems in such a situation. Problems like this can be extremely disturbing during natural infection tests in lab environments. It is an example of Murphy's Law when the whole world is infected with a particular worm-which fails to work in the lab environment.

Nevertheless, the technique seems to be efficient in the real world, and many successful worm attacks are the proof. For example, the W32/Mydoom@mm worm became extremely widespread in early 2004. Mydoom parsed files for e-mails with the following extensions: HTM, SHT, PHP, ASP, DBX, TBB, ADB, PL, WAB, and TXT. Computer worms use heuristics to figure out whether a particular string is a possible e-mail address. One possible heuristic is to look for mailto: strings in HTML files and assume it is followed by an e-mail address. Occasionally, the size of the domain name is limited. For example, somebody@a.com might not be accepted by worms such as W32/Klez.H as a valid e-mail address, because "a.com" is too short to be good (although someone might configure a local network using such domain name). In addition, some worms target recipients with a specific language such as Hungarian and, to trick the user to execute the worm, they check the TLD (top-level domain) of e-mail addresses as suggested. For example, the Zafi.A worm sends itself to e-mail addresses that have ".hu" (Hungarian) as their TLD. Sircam worm searches for e-mail addresses in Internet Explorer's Cache directory, the user's Personal directory, and the directory that contains the Windows Address Books in files whose names begins with sho, get, or hot, or whose suffix is HTM or WAB.

Attackers have long introduced their creations in internet newsgroups. In 1996 the abuse of the News Net became very intense. As a result, researchers of the Dr. Solomon antivirus team decided to create a service called Virus Patrol to scan Usenet messages for known and possibly unknown malware that was continuously planted in such messages. Virus Patrol was introduced in December 1996. NNTP can be used in a number of malicious ways. For example, an attacker might be able to use a news server reader to build a large local database with the e-mail addresses of millions of people. The attacker can use this database to help the initial fast propagation of the worm by running the worm on a system that hosts the database.

This is a common technique of spammers, and it is suspected that worms such as the W32/Sobig family were populated using such techniques. The newsgroupbased e-mail collector is not entirely unknown in Win32 viruses. In fact, the very first known Win32 virus that used e-mail to propagate itself used an NNTP collector. W32/Parvo was introduced by the infamous virus writer GriYo of the 29A group in late 1998. Not surprisingly, just like many other GriYo viruses, Parvo also used polymorphism to infect PE files, but it also became the first virus to integrate an SMTP mass-mailing engine. Parvo was years ahead of its time, written in pure Assembly resulting in a 15KB virus body.

W32/Parvo used several newsgroups to collect e-mail addresses, but apparently a minor problem limited its spread. Parvo randomly tried to connect to two possible news servers: talia.ibernet.es or diana.ibernet.es. These servers, however, were not available to everyone at the time. Thus Parvo's newsgroup-based e-mail collector was limited to work "inside the borders" of Spain.

Parvo connects on port 119/TCP (NNTP) to one of the preceding servers and starts to communicate. The attacker prepared three different e-mail messages with content that he expected to be catchy enough for the selected audiences of three different newsgroups. Parvo's first message targets frequent readers of hacking-related newsgroups, such as alt.bio.hackers, alt.hacker, alt.hackers, alt.hackers.malicious, and so on. The second message is sent to a subset of this newsgroup list. Finally, the third message targeted visitors to erotic newsgroups, such as alt.binaries.erotica, alt.binaries.erotica.pornstar, and so on. To find e-mail addresses in newsgroups, Parvo uses the group command to join to a group randomly and then uses the head and next commands a random number of times to pick a message randomly. Finally, it extracts the e-mail address from the header of the randomly selected message, sends itself in e-mail to the target, and repeats the process.

Attackers also can search for e-mail addresses using search engines. This is a relatively simple task that can help the attacker gain quick access to a large number of e-mails. The first such worms appeared that utilised popular search engines such as Google, Lycos, Yahoo!, and Altavista to harvest email addresses. For example, the W32/Mydoom.M@mm worm used this technique successfully, and according to Google, it caused minor DoS attacks against its servers.

Alternatively, a computer worm can capture e-mail addresses from outgoing messages. Even if a particular e-mail address is not saved anywhere on the system, when the user sends a message to a particular address, the worm can send a message to the same address. The Happy99 worm was the first to use this method.

Of course, there can be many variations of e-mail address harvesting and worm propagation. For example, the Linux/Slapper worm is capable of harvesting e-mail addresses and providing them to the attacker based on his request via a remotecontrol interface. Then another worm might be created by the attacker to use the database of harvested e-mail addresses to propagate to a large number of machines very rapidly-without requiring a large set of initial infections to harvest an efficient number of e-mail addresses. Even more likely, the attacker can use the collected e-mail addresses to spam targets.

Network Share Enumeration Attacks

Probably the simplest method to find other nodes on the network quickly is to enumerate the network for remote systems. Windows systems are especially vulnerable to such attacks because of their rich support for finding other machines with simple interfaces. Computer viruses such as W32/Funlove used the enumeration principle to infect files on remote targets. These attacks caused major outbreaks at large corporations around the world. Several computer worms have minor implementation problems and become overly successful at finding networked resources, including shared network printer resources. This happens because not all worms pay attention to the type of resources they enumerate, which can lead to accidental printing on the network printers. Indeed, bogus worms print random-looking binary garbage on the printer, which is in fact the code of the worm. W32/Bugbear and W32/ Wangy are examples of computer worms that accidentally target network printers with such an attack.

The success of this kind of worm usually depends on the trusted relationship between systems. However, there are additional contributors:

- *Blank passwords*: Many default installations of systems are vulnerable to attacks because they do not have a default password set for administrativelevel access on shared resources.
- *Weak passwords-dictionary attacks:* Weak passwords were a target of computer worms as early as 1988, starting with the Morris worm. However, password dictionary attacks on Windows systems did not become popular until 2003, with the sudden outbreak of worms like BAT/Mumu. Surprisingly, Mumu carried a relatively short password list that includes password, passwd, admin, pass, 123, 1234, 12345, 123456, and a blank password. Most likely, its success is related to the blank passwords on administrator accounts.
- *Vulnerabilities related to the handling of passwords*: The W32/Opaserv worm appeared in September of 2002 and became infamous for its attacks against systems that were otherwise protected with strong passwords, but that shared network resources on vulnerable Windows installations. Specifically, Opaserv exploited the vulnerability described in the MS00-072 security bulletin, which affected Microsoft Windows 95/98 and Me systems. This vulnerability, known as the share-level password vulnerability, allows access to network shares using the first character of the password, no

matter how long the password is. The number of systems that share network resources on the internet without being protected by a personal firewall is overwhelming, which allows Opaserv easy access to writeable shared resources.

– *Password-capturing attacks to gain domain administrator-level rights*: In Windows networks, domain administrators have the right to read and write any files on any Windows machine on the network, unless specifically forbidden. On NT-based systems, domain administrators can also remotely execute programs on the fly and execute commands that require higher privilege levels than those of a regular user on the network.

These features make remote management possible, but at the same time they open up a whole new set of security problems. Gaining domain administrator rights is not trivial. However, a worm could do this easily if given enough time. A worm could spread through traditional channels, constantly sniffing the local network segment with traditional TCP/IP sniffing techniques. After detecting the domain administrator credentials being transferred in the network segment, it logs the domain administrator's username and password hash.

NT-based networks do not broadcast the password in plain text; they run it through a one-way hash function first. The function cannot be reversed, so the password cannot be gathered directly from the hash. Instead, the worm could execute a brute-force attack to exhaust every possible password combination. It could run every password (A, AA, AAA, AAAA, and so on) through the same one-way function and compare the result. If they match, the password has been found. Alternatively, the worm could use a dictionary attack to find passwords as well. With a strong password, this process might take days to accomplish, but a typical NT password takes less than a week to crack on a typical Windows workstation from a single Pentium system.'Assuming that the worm could communicate with other compromised nodes, it could introduce workload balancing between the compromised nodes to share the work, making the cracking process even faster.

After the worm has cracked the NT domain administrator password, it owns the network and can do anything. Specifically, it can copy itself to any other Windows machine in the network. On NT-based machines, it can even start itself automatically with high access rights. Such a worm could also change the domain administrator password and the local administrator passwords to make itself more difficult to stop. We first projected the feasibility of such attacks on NT domains with Mikko Hypponen back in 1997. At about the same time, tools such as L0phtCrack appeared to fulfill the sniffing and breaking of password hashes on NT domains. The authors of L0phtCrack demonstrated that long passwords can be often weaker than short ones when challenged with dictionary attacks. In fact, the hashing algorithm of passwords on NT domains splits long passwords to seven character chunks, helping L0phtCrack crack the password more quickly. Nevertheless, computer worms with built-in network sniffing to crack passwords have not been discovered so far.

Network Scanning

Several computer worms construct random IP addresses to attack other nodes on the network. By analysing the scanning algorithm of the worm, someone might be able to make predictions about the worm's propagation speed on the network. Evidently, an attacker can scan the entire internet from a single machine, building IP addresses in a sequential manner and carefully ignoring invalid IP address ranges. This technique allows the attacker to build a "hit list" to systems that might be vulnerable against a particular attack. To do that, the attacker typically fingerprints the remote systems just enough to suspect that the target may be vulnerable. In many cases, the fingerprinting is strongly related to a successful exploitation. The hit list method is one of the theoretical backgrounds for so-called Warhol worms. Warhol worms can infect 90% of all vulnerable systems on the entire internet in less than 15 minutes. Network worms can also scan for remote systems, generating random IP addresses but using a predefined table of network classes.

Backdoor-Compromised System Attacks

Although most computer worms do not intentionally attack an already compromised system, some computer worms use other backdoor interfaces to propagate themselves. The W32/Borm worm was among the first computer worms to attack a backdoor-compromised remote system. W32/Borm cannot infect any other systems than those already compromised with Back Orifice (a fairly popular backdoor among attackers). Back Orifice supports a remote command interface that uses an encrypted channel between a client and the Back Orifice server installed on the compromised system. Borm utilises a network-scanning and fingerprinting function to locate Back Orifice-compromised systems. The worm attacks a compromised system using the following simple steps:

1. It randomly generates an IP address and actively scans using Back Orifice's BO_PING command to see whether the remote system is compromised. To initiate any meaningful communication, the worm needs to know Back Orifice's magic password, which is

*!*QWTY?. The header of the communication data is encrypted with simple encryption, which is required by the Back Orifice server. Borm properly encrypts the data before it sends it to the randomly generated IP address on port 31337/UDP used by Back Orifice. If the remote node answers the BO_PING command, the worm proceeds to the next step. Otherwise, it generates other IP addresses to attack.

2. Borm sends a BO_HTTP_ENABLE command to the server.
3. In turn, this command instructs Back Orifice to create a virtual HTTP server on the compromised host. The worm instructs Back Orifice to use port 12345/TCP to establish an HTTP proxy on the compromised system.
4. Next, the worm connects and uploads itself in MIME-encoded format to the server.
5. Finally, the worm runs the uploaded executable on the server by sending a BO_PROCESS_SPAWN command. This will run the worm on the remote machine so it can start to scan for other Back Orifice systems from the newly infected node.

W32/Borm was among a flurry of computer worms that appeared in 2001. Other worms that utilised backdoor interfaces in this time frame included Nimda, which took advantage of a backdoor that was previously opened by a CodeRed II infection, and the W32/Leaves worm, which got in the wild by attacking SubSeven Trojan-compromised systems. Borm was a creation of the Brazilian virus writer, Vecna.

Peer-to-Peer Attacks

Peer-to-peer attacks are an increasingly popular computer worm technique that not require advanced scanning methods on the computer network. Instead, such worms simply make a copy of themselves to a shared P2P folder on the disk. Anything that is available in a P2P download folder is searchable by other users on the P2P network.In fact, some computer worms even create the shared folder in case the user only wants to search the P2P network for content instead of sharing similar content with others.

Although this attack is similar to a Trojan installation, rather than recursive propagation, users of the P2P network will find the network-shared content easily and run the malicious code on their systems to complete the infection cycle. Some P2P worms, such as W32/Maax, will infect files in the P2P folder. The most common infection technique is the overwriting method, but prepender and even appender infections have also been seen. P2P clients such as KaZaA, KaZaA Lite, Limewire, Morpheus, Grokster, BearShare, and Edonkey among others are common targets of malicious code. P2P networks are an increasingly popular way to exchange digital music; they are hard to regulate because they are not centralised.

Instant Messaging Attacks

Instant messaging attacks originated in the abuse of the mIRC /DCC Send command. This command can be used to send a file to users connected to a particular discussion channel. Normally, attackers modify a local script file, such as script.ini used by mIRC to instruct the instant messaging client to send a file to a recipient any time a new participant joins a discussion. Modern implementations of IRC (Internet Relay Chat) worms can connect dynamically to an IRC client and send messages that trick the recipient into executing a link or an attachment. In this way, the attacker can avoid modifying any local files. For example, the W32/Choke worm uses the MSN Messenger API to send itself to other instant messaging participants as a "shooter game". Although several instant messenger software programs require the user to click a button to send a file, worms can enumerate the dialog boxes and "click" the button, so the actual user does not have to click. It is also expected that computer worms will exploit buffer overflow vulnerabilities in instant messenger software. For example, certain versions of AOL Instant Messenger software allow remote execution of arbitrary code via a long argument in a game request function.

SMTP Attacks

As Microsoft strengthened Outlook's security to protect end users better against worm attacks, computer worm authors quickly started to use more and more SMTP-based attacks. The first such major worldwide outbreak was caused by the Sircam worm in July 2001 and was followed by the infamous W32/Nimda worm in September 2001. Smaller outbreaks had signaled the problem earlier, with the in-the-wild appearance of W32/ExploreZip in June 1999. Sircam avoids relying on an e-mail program by getting the SMTP information directly from the Registry.

Using a hard-coded list of SMTP IP addresses is a common technique for computer worms, but usually this trick quickly overloads the particular set of servers once the worm is sufficiently widespread. Typically, such worms take off their SMTP servers with a DoS attack very quickly. Thanks to implementation mistakes and bugs, it took a little while before SMTP worms could take their real place. Before Sircam, most worms lacked some important detail in their spreading mechanism.

Worm Code Transfer

Computer worms also differ how they propagate the worm's code from one system to another. Most computer worms simply propagate their main body as an attachment in an e-mail. However, other types of worms utilise different methods, such as injected code and shellcode techniques in conjunction with exploit code, to attack another system. E-mail can be encoded in various ways, such as UU, BASE64 (MIME), and so on. However, the UU-encoded attachments are not very reliable over the internet because UU uses some special characters whose interpretation depends on the context. Nowadays, most e-mail clients use MIME-encoded attachments by default-and that is how most e-mail worms' SMTP client engines transfer themselves to new targets. Script e-mail worms usually send attachments encoded according to the settings of the e-mail client on the compromised system.

Computer worms also can send links to executables hosted elsewhere, such as a single Web site, a set of Web sites, or an FTP location. The actual message on IRC or in e-mail might not have any malicious content in it directly-but infects indirectly. One problem with this kind of attack is the possibility of an accidental DoS attack against the system that hosts the worm's code. Another potential pitfall is that the defender can easily contact internet service providers to request they disconnect such sites, preventing further propagation of the computer worm. Tricky worms send links with the IP address of an already compromised system. First, the worm compromises a machine and opens a crude Web server on the system. Then it sends messages to other users, using the IP address of the machine with the port on which the worm itself is listening for a GET request. In this way, the worm attack becomes peer-to-peer. Such computer worms might be able to bypass content filtering easily if the contentfiltering rule is based on attachment filtering.

On UNIX-like systems, commands such as rsh, rlogin, rcp, and rexec can be used directly by computer worms.

Using such commands, worms can execute themselves on remote systems if the attacked system is not secured or if the password is guessed with a dictionary attack or similar method. Usually, such worms make a copy of their code directly to the remote system and execute themselves via the remote execution facilities.

On Windows systems, worms like JS/Spida can take advantage of vulnerable Microsoft SQL servers. Spida scans for remote Microsoft SQL server systems on port 1433 and tries to execute itself remotely with the following assumptions:

– The Microsoft SQL server runs in Administrative mode.

– The "sa" Microsoft SQL server account has no password set.

The worm takes advantage of the xp_cmdshell function to execute system commands to run the worm on the remote machine.

A more advanced attack requires exploitation of a target with direct code injection over the network. As traditional buffer overflows are getting more difficult to exploit, attackers are increasingly interested in exploiting server-side vulnerabilities related to a lack of input validation. For example, the Perl/Santy worm utilises Google to find vulnerable Web sites and runs its own Perl script via a vulnerability in the phpBB bulletin board software. This worm successfully defaced tens of thousands of Web sites on December 21 of 2004. Depending on the thread model of the vulnerable target server, one of the following actions will happen:

– A new thread is created at the start of the server.

– A new thread is created upon each incoming request.

Furthermore, depending on the context of the hijacked thread, the worm

- Runs in SYSTEM context with high privileges.
- Runs in the context of a user with either high or low privileges that the worm might be able to escalate.

These preconditions are often reflected in the worm's operation. When, for example, W32/Slammer exploits a vulnerable Microsoft SQL server, the worm hijacks a thread that was executed at the start of the server. Thus the operations associated with the hijacked thread will be paralysed because new incoming requests will not be resolved. In addition, the server process and the entire system is heavily overloaded because the worm never stops sending itself to new targets.

An example of the second type of attack is W32/CodeRed. CodeRed exploits Microsoft IIS server via a malformed GET request. When the server receives the GET request, it executes a new thread to process it. The worm hijacks that particular thread and creates 100 new threads (300 in some variants) in the vulnerable server process. This kind of computer worm needs to avoid infecting the target a second time because the worm could exploit the target multiple times, causing the target to be overloaded shortly after the initial outbreak. In addition, computer worms that counterattack each other can also benefit from this condition because they can utilise the same exploit as their opponent.

Another class of computer worms utilise shell code on the target machine. The basic idea is to run a command prompt on the remote system, such as cmd.exe (on Windows) or /bin/sh (on UNIX) via the exploit code. Consider The worm follows these steps:.

1. It injects code into a remote process and binds a specific port to the process. The exploited process starts to listen on the port.
2. The worm attempts to connect to the listening port.
3. If the connection to the port is successful, the previously injected shellcode executes a command prompt and binds that process to the same port that the attacker is using.
4. Finally, the worm can start to send commands to the shell.

Shellcode-based attacks are typically more common on UNIX systems than on Windows systems. A few variations exist, such as back-connecting shellcode and shellcode that reuses an existing connection. Back-connecting shellcode immediately attempts to connect the target with the attacker by establishing a TCP connection from the target to the attacker's machine. The advantage of this method is that it allows machines behind a firewall to "connect-out" to the attacker system.

Update Mechanisms

Computer worms can be classified according to their update strategies. An early example of this is W95/Babylonia, a Windows Help and PE infector and self-mailer that was discovered on December 6, 1999. Babylonia was posted to the alt.crackers internet newsgroup as a Windows Help file named serialz.hlp, which appeared to be a list of serial numbers for commercial software. This Help file was launched by many people who activated the virus on their systems. When executed, the virus creates a downloader component that looks for updates on a Web site. First, the downloader reads the content of a text file called virus.txt stored on the Web site. This text file lists a few filenames, such as dropper.dat, greetz.dat, ircworm.dat, and poll.dat. These files use a special plug-in file format with a header that starts with the identifier VMOD (which stands for virus module).

Realising the weaknesses of a single Web site-based update system, Vecna decided to use alternated update channels and strong cryptography to authenticate the updates. The W95/Hybris worm was released in late 2000. It was an unusually large project of several top virus writers from around the world: Brazilian, Spanish, Russian, and French virus writers were all part of the large team that developed it. Hybris uses 1,023-bit RSA signing to deliver its update modules to infected systems. It also uses a 128-bit hash function to protect the updates against attacks. The hash function uses XTEA. XTEA is in the public domain, written by David Wheeler and Roger Needham. The RSA library for Hybris was written by the infamous Russian virus writer, Zombie.

Note the interesting selection for XTEA instead of TEA, which was previously found weak by cryptographers John Kelsey, Bruce Schneier, and David Wagner many years ago at CRYPTO 1996. In fact, TEA was used as a hash function in the security of the second version of the Microsoft Xbox. This weakness was leveraged a day later after its announcement by a team headed by Andy Green to break the security of the Xbox scheme by flipping bits in Xbox's FLASH ROM code that allowed a jump instruction to branch to RAM.

The idea of the Hybris worm is to encrypt the updates with XTEA and sign the update files with RSA on the attacker's system. The attacker creates a secret key and a corresponding public key. He puts the public key into the virus, and the XTEA encryption/decryption keys are delivered with the module-but are signed with a 1,023-bit RSA secret key. This is called a hybrid signing technique, which makes the process more efficient. Instead of using a single 128-bit key, Hybris uses 8 XTEA keys, one of which is a hash computed about the plug-in and 7 other 128-bit keys that are set randomly. First, a 128-bit hash of the module is calculated using XTEA. This value will be used as one of eight 128-bit encryption keys to encrypt the entire module using a 64-bit XTEA block cipher. The block cipher applies the eight 128-bit keys to each consecutive 64-bit block of the plug-in. Each 64-bit block is encrypted with one 128-bit key. Thus the first 64-bit block is encrypted with the first key in the set, the second 64-bit block is encrypted with the second 128-bit key until the keys wrap around: The 9 block is encrypted with the first key again, and so on.

Signing allows the worm instances to check if the update files were distributed by the virus writer. Thus the RSA algorithm is used to prevent changes to plug-ins or to create new plug-ins without specifically involving the attacker who holds the secret key. The worm uses the public key corresponding to the secret key of the attacker to validate the signed XTEA key and verifies that the hash is correct to avoid forgery attacks. Although the updates are encrypted, the algorithm uses a symmetric key so the modules can be decrypted by anyone, in the same way as the worm decrypts them. The attacker is protected against any manipulations that could occur to update modules. Thus it is not feasible to distribute an update that could kill the worm without the secret key of the virus author unless, of course, there is some implementation error discovered that commonly occurs in cryptography. There were up to 20 known modules (so-called Muazzins) for Hybris. However, there were more than 32 different versions of these in circulation. After encrypting and signing the module, the attacker encoded the module to send it to the alt.comp.virus newsgroup. Infected systems, which were all looking for the modules, downloaded and decrypted them using their public keys. Although the initial update Web site was quickly disabled, the attacker had the opportunity to send out new updates in newsgroups. Infected nodes propagated the modules back to the newsgroups, so all infected nodes had a chance to get the updates.

Several computer worms open up a port on the compromised system and implement an interface to execute arbitrary files on the compromised machine. The attacker can use this interface to update the worm's code from one version to another. For instance, the W32/Mydoom worm opens a TCP port in the range of 3127 to 3198 and waits for a connection, implementing a simple protocol. Essentially, Mydoom's code is updated similarly to a backdoor-based propagation technique. The attacker needs to scan for systems that have a port open and can send an executable to the target that will be executed on the remote node. The first few versions of Mydoom did not implement any security mechanism for their update protocol. Not surprisingly, worms such as W32/Doomjuice, W32/Beagle, and W32/Welchia attacked Mydoom-compromised systems by taking advantage of the insecure update mechanism.

Controlling the Worm

Attackers often want to control their creations remotely, for example, to execute a DoS attack against a selected target or to control the propagation of the worm to new systems. The most obvious technique is based on the use of a backdoor feature built into the worm that communicates directly with a particular host. However, other known techniques centrally control the worm, such as via IRC or Windows domain mail-slots. Some of the variants of this worm only propagate the infection to new targets whenever the attacker sends a ".spread" signal to an IRC server into a discussion channel of the worm itself. When the attacker sends the ".spread" signal, the already compromised systems look for new targets to infect. Techniques include e-mail, instant messaging, and SubSeven backdoor-compromised nodes attack. In addition, the attacker can execute a DoS attack against any target. The target of the DoS attack is unknown to the compromised systems until the attacker sends the command. Then the compromised nodes turn against the specified target and execute various kinds of flooding methods. Hence the name of the worm, which is Floodnet spelled backwards. This kind of remote control-based worm propagation is often confusing for junior antivirus researchers.

Some computer worms implement a virtual network between infected nodes to establish communication and control operations. The Linux/Slapper worm is an example of this kind of computer worm. Slapper uses the UDP protocol and port 2002 on each infected node. When the worm infects a new target, it passes the attacker's IP address to the target system. Then each node receives the IP addresses of all other nodes and keeps these in a list. Whenever a new IP address is introduced, all other nodes receive the update via this special virtual network, which uses TCP-like (stateful) features to ensure that the information arrives at the target correctly. The infected nodes select a random set of other machines to broadcast the updated information on the network. This is called a broadcast segmentation technique.

The remote control interface of Linux/Slapper is very advanced. The code is borrowed from the BSD/Scalper worm, which was based on a previous attacker tool. Just like Scalper, Slapper implements a hierarchical network structure that keeps track of systems the worm has infected. Slapper supports a large set of commands that implement UDP flood, TCP SYN flood, IPv6 SYN flood, and DNS standard query flood DoS attacks; it also supports the execution of arbitrary commands on the compromised nodes.

3

Spamming, Spoofing and Stalking

SPAMMING

Spamming is the abuse of any electronic communications medium to send unsolicited messages in bulk. In the popular eye, the most common form of spam is that delivered in e-mail as a form of commercial advertising. However, over the short history of electronic media, people have spammed for many purposes other than the commercial, and in many media other than e-mail.

Spammers have developed a variety of spamming techniques, which vary by media: e-mail spam, instant messaging spam, usenet newsgroup spam, Web search engines spam, spam in blogs, and mobile phone messaging spam. Spamming is economically viable because advertisers have effectively no operating costs beyond the management of their mailing lists. Because the barrier to entry is so low, the volume of unsolicited mail has produced other costs which are borne by the public and by internet service providers, which must add extra capacity to cope with the deluge.

Generally, spam has some or all of the following characteristics:

– Return address is not valid. If you try replying to spam e-mail, you will get a delivery error.

- Forged headers. To hide the origin of the e-mail, routing headers are usually forged, which makes it very difficult to trace persistent spammers.
- The identity of the recipient is irrelevant because the e-mail is valid for many other recipients.
- Dictionary attack address. If the 'To' address line is examined, you may see different variants of the recipient's e-mail addresses.
- Subject line has no bearing on the content of the e-mail. Bulk e-mailers use programs to randomly generate characters in the subject line in order to bypass spam filters.
- E-mail content is of a dubious nature.
- Unsubscribe does not work in spam e-mail. If you try to unsubscribe from spam e-mail, it is often the case that the link does not work, or opens up an advertisement's web site. What it does confirm however is the legitimacy of your e-mail address, which would be duly added to another spam list of verified e-mail addresses.
- May contain hidden scripts. If spam contains HTML, it may contain hidden JavaScript, which can open up web sites and activate advertisement popup windows.

Here is a sampling of the top spam e-mails currently roaming the internet:

- "URGENT AND CONFIDENTIAL". This is the Nigerian spam asking e-mail recipients for bank account information in order to deposit large amounts of money from Nigeria.
- "GET A FREE PASS TO THOUSANDS OF XXX SITES!" Spam e-mail advertising pornographic web sites.

- "Protect Your Computer Against Viruses for $9.95". An offer for a cheap antivirus software program.
- "Verification Department". This is a credit card scam e-mail that purports to be from a credit card company offering the e-mail recipient the opportunity to receive a credit card, irrespective of credit history or employment status.
- "Online Auction Marketing Secrets!" Another spam scam that claims to reveal secrets to online auctioning success.
- "Printer Cartridges—Save up to 80%—free shipping offer". Spam e-mail to sell printer cartridges with enormous savings.

Spam has become an industry and the economics of this fledgling industry are impressive even when the financial dealings of bulk e-mail companies, who operate within the confines of the law, are excluded. Spam has become an industry, mainly due to the low cost involved in sending spam. The average spam costs the spammer 0.00032 cents, so sending bulk e-mail is very cheap. However, the reason why it is so cheap is because of the notion of cost shifting, which means the cost to the recipient is greater than the cost to the sender.

A spammer can use a simple modem to send e-mail to thousands of internet users. The cost to the recipient could include resources such as processor time, disk storage, bandwidth, anti-virus software, and spam filtering software. If you have a finite storage space with an ISP, spam e-mail may fill up your allocated space and block legitimate e-mail. The cost to the ISP is passed on to the consumer. A single piece of spam e-mail from source to destination could pass through a number of ISPs along the way, with the burden of delivery placed on the ISP.

On the other hand, these very same ISPs sign lucrative contracts with known spammers. Under the guise of not regulating content, some backbone providers are happy to sell 45Mbps DS3 circuits to bulk e-mailers. The price tag for one of these circuits from a Tier-1 provider could range anywhere from $30,000–$40,000 per month. A well-known Louisiana-based spammer claims to use three of these circuits in order to send 84 Million bulk e-mails a day.

Spam does not only target e-mail inboxes. Mobile phones, Blackberry pagers, PDAs (Personal Digital Assistants) and other mobile devices are also targets of spam. If a company whose sales force communicates with each other and gain access to their corporate e-mail using Blackberry pagers, then the cost of spam is substantial. With these systems, the user is charged by the amount of bandwidth that is consumed, so each spam message has a varying monitory cost. Spam has also begun to invade other wireless platforms where the user is charged on a per-message basis.

The spam industry can be regarded as those who make a business out of sending spam and those who business revolve around anti-spam software and services. It is interesting to see how the spam industry mimics other marketing strategies. During the holiday seasons of Christmas and Thanksgiving in 2002, there was a marked increase in the amount of spam being detected, corresponding to the marketing blitz strategies of consumer industries in an attempt to encourage people to spend more during these lucrative periods.

There are organisations that support the rights of spammers to send bulk e-mail. In the United States, the Direct Marketing Association (DMA) is a well-funded lobbying group that maintains a pro-spam stance. The

DMA believe that any non-porn, non-fraud bulk email should not be classified as spam. The association represents approximately 5,000 companies that send both postal and electronic mail. At its conference in October 2002, it was reported that 2/3 of its members generated increased sales due to e-mail marketing. Some of the members stated that an e-mail campaign could result in up to 12 times the response rate of ordinary postal mail. With statistics like this, it is no wonder why advertisers find this medium to be very attractive.

Some spammers operate out in the open as registered companies, where they pay taxes and generally adhere to accepted business practices. One Ohio-based spammer in the United States has 60 employees and yearly sales of $12 million. They churn out 5 billion spam e-mails every month for everything from nutritional supplements to houseimprovements. The owner of the company asserts that they have hundreds of corporate clients, including publicly traded companies. Some companies argue that organisations like AOL want to keep advertising revenues to themselves and stopping bulk e-mail to the millions of AOL users is an unfair business practice. Forrester Research estimates that corporations will spend approximately $6 billion on e-mail marketing in 2005. Traditional companies such as Ford and Procter & Gamble are joining new age companies such as Amazon.com in the highly lucrative e-mail marketing strategy. E-mail facilitates access to the global marketplace and allows companies to achieve sales in far-reaching places of the world. It is simple for bulk e-mail recipients to click through to a company's web site and make a purchase.

The European Union estimates the cost of spam worldwide at $8—$10 billion annually. An anti-spam industry has evolved with many companies hopeful to reap the rewards of the cash injected into the industry by eager venture capitalists. The industry can be categorised into two main areas of concentration: anti-spam software and anti-spam services. Some businesses are capable of offering both solutions, and are comparable to other companies in the software/services industry. Their offerings are geared to the large enterprises, service providers and educational institutions, right down to the home user. Spam analysis can be very costly in terms of time and processor usage, and if it is performed on the contents of every e-mail message, then there is a noticeable delivery overhead for organisations with substantial numbers of users. Mail throughput is very important to many companies. This in turn leads to competition within the anti-spam industry to produce faster and more reliable filters. There were approximately 200 businesses in the anti-spam industry at the start of 2003 with more to follow, as the projected market is expected to grow to $181 million in 3 years. The irony with the anti-spam industry is that some of the companies that offer anti-spam solutions have used spam to develop business. At least two of these companies acquired spam mail lists and sent e-mail to addresses on the lists offering their anti-spam services.

E-mail Spamming

E-mail spam is a subset of spam that involves sending nearly identical messages to thousands (or millions) of recipients. Perpetrators of such spam (spammers) often harvest addresses of prospective recipients from Usenet postings or from web pages, obtain them from databases, or simply guess them by using common names and domains. By popular definition, spam occurs without the permission of the recipients. As the recipient directly bears the cost of delivery, storage, and processing, one could regard spam as the electronic equivalent of "postage-due" junk mail. However, the Direct Marketing Association will point to the existence of "legitimate" e-mail marketing.

Most commentators classify e-mail-based marketing campaigns where the recipient has "opted in" to receive the marketer's message as "legitimate". Spammers frequently engage in deliberate fraud to send out their messages. Spammers often use false names, addresses, phone numbers, and other contact information to set up "disposable" accounts at various internet service providers. They also often use falsified or stolen credit card numbers to pay for these accounts. This allows them to move quickly from one account to the next as the host ISPs discover and shut down each one.

Spammers cannot completely spoof e-mail delivery chains, since the receiving mailserver records the actual connection from the last mailserver's IP address. To counter this, some spammers forge additional delivery headers to make it appear as if the e-mail had previously traversed many legitimate servers. But even when the fake headers are identified, tracing an e-mail message's route is usually fruitless. Many ISPs have thousands of customers, and identifying spammers is tedious and generally not considered worth the effort. Spammers frequently seek out and make use of vulnerable third-party systems such as open mail relays and open proxy servers. The SMTP system, used to send e-mail across the internet, forwards mail from one server to another; mail servers that ISPs run commonly require some form of authentication that the user is a customer of that ISP. Open relays, however, do not properly check who is using the mail server and pass all mail to the destination address, making it quite a bit harder to track down spammers. Increasingly, spammers use networks of virus-infected Windows PCs to send their spam.

Spoofing can have serious consequences for legitimate e-mail users. Not only can their e-mail inboxes get clogged up with "undeliverable" e-mails in addition to volumes of spam, they can mistakenly be identified as a spammer. Not only may they receive irate e-mail from spam victims, but their ISP may terminate their service for spamming. Sending spam violates the Acceptable Use Policy (AUP) of almost all internet service providers, and can lead to the termination of the sender's account. Many jurisdictions, such as the United States of America, which regulates via the CAN-SPAM Act of 2003, regard spamming as a crime or as an actionable tort. Article 13 of the European Union Directive on Privacy and Electronic Communications provides that the EU member states shall take appropriate measures to ensure that unsolicited communications for the purposes of direct marketing are not allowed either without the consent of the subscribers concerned or in respect of subscribers who do not wish to receive these communications, the choice between these options to be determined by national legislation.

Accessing privately owned computer resources without the owner's permission counts as illegal under computer crime statutes in most nations. Deliberate spreading of computer viruses is also illegal in the United States and elsewhere. Thus, some of spammers' most common behaviors are criminal quite independently of the legal status of spamming per se. Even before the advent of laws specifically banning or regulating spamming, spammers have been successfully prosecuted under computer fraud and abuse laws for wrongfully using others' computers.

Computer users can avoid e-mail spam in several ways:

- End-users can use automated e-mail filtering on their own computers.
- System administrators can use appropriate tools to trap e-mail spam at the mail server level, either by use of software or special appliances.

- Spam can be reported to appropriate ISP so that the spamming can be stopped.
- By giving out one's ISP e-mail address only to closely trusted acquaintances, friends, and relatives, and using web based e-mail services for everyone else.
- By ensuring that those acquaintances, friends and relatives who have been trusted with one's e-mail address do not include the person who wants to avoid spam's e-mail address in the "To" or "CC" fields when sending several copies of an e-mail to ensure that, when such e-mails are forwarded, to avoid one's e-mail addresses from appearing in an ammassing list of e-mail addresses
- By creating a unique e-mail address for each person or site you wish to communicate with. This can be done using an online mail forwarding service, or with administrative access to your own e-mail server. If spam is received on one of these addresses, you immediately know who leaked or sold your address to spammers, and you can also cancel the affected e-mail address.
- End-users can take precautions to avoid needlessly publicising their e-mail addresses or protect them from e-mail harvesting by spam bots, such as by using e-mail forms that do not display the address in the webpage code, or by address munging.
- Using anti-virus and anti-spyware programs with regularly updated definitions to avoid having their computers hijacked and used as spammer tools.
- Users are also advised to configure their e-mail clients to disable rich content features such as HTML mail and automatic downloading of images. Downloaded images can be used by spammers to identify valid e-mail addresses.

- By periodically performing an internet search for one's own email address, and if necessary getting the appropriate website administrator to remove it.

Anti-spam programmers have released several tools—intended for both end users and for systems administrators—which automate the highlighting, removal or filtering of e-mail spam by scanning through incoming and outgoing e-mails in search of traits typical of spam. Modern anti-spam systems are usually very effective at protecting you from spam. Like other forms of theft, spam should be reported to the appropriate people so that it can be stopped. Services, such as spamcop, make this easy to do. While this may not immediately decrease the amount of spam you receive significantly, it will reduce the amount of spam that everyone receives. The best way to avoid spam involves avoiding making one's e-mail address available to spammers, directly or indirectly.

Basic computer literacy should include an understanding of the basics of spamming and spam avoidance. One should never reply to a spam e-mail, or click an "opt-out" link. Users should not reveal their e-mail addresses on porn, warez and other shady sites.If a web site requests registration in order to allow useful operations, such as posting in internet forums, a user may give a temporary disposable address—set up and used only for such a purpose—periodically deleting such temporary e-mail accounts from their e-mail servers.

The Process of Spamming

In order to send spam, spammers need to obtain the e-mail addresses of the intended recipients. Toward this end, both spammers themselves and list merchants gather huge lists of potential e-mail addresses. Since spam is, by definition, unsolicited, this address harvesting is done without the consent of the address owners. As a consequence, spammers' address lists are remarkably inaccurate. A single spam run may target tens of millions of possible addresses – many of which are invalid, malformed, or undeliverable. Spam differs from other forms of direct marketing in many ways, one of them being that it costs no more to send to a larger number of recipients than a smaller number. For this reason, there is little pressure upon spammers to limit the number of addresses targeted in a spam run, or to restrict it to persons likely to be interested. One consequence of this fact is that many people receive spam written in languages they cannot read – a good deal of spam sent to English-speaking recipients is in Chinese or Korean, for instance. Likewise, lists of addresses sold for use in spam frequently contain malformed addresses, duplicate addresses, and addresses of role accounts such as postmaster.

Spammers may harvest e-mail addresses from a number of sources. A popular method uses e-mail addresses which their owners have published for other purposes. Usenet posts, especially those in archives such as Google Groups, frequently yield addresses. Simply searching the Web for pages with addresses – such as corporate staff directories – can yield thousands of addresses, most of them deliverable. Spammers have also subscribed to discussion mailing lists for the purpose of gathering the addresses of posters. The DNS and WHOIS systems require the publication of technical contact information for all internet domains; spammers have illegally trawled these resources for e-mail addresses. Many spammers utilise programs called web spiders to find e-mail addresses on web pages. A recent, controversial tactic, called "e-pending", involves the appending of e-mail addresses to direct-marketing databases. Direct marketers normally obtain lists of prospects from sources such as magazine subscriptions and customer lists. By searching the Web and other resources for e-mail addresses corresponding to the names and street addresses in their records, direct marketers can send targeted spam e-mail. However, as with most spammer "targeting", this is imprecise; users have reported, for instance, receiving solicitations to mortgage their house at a specific street address – with the address being clearly a business address including mail stop and office number.

Spammers sometimes use various means to confirm addresses as deliverable. For instance, including a Web bug in a spam message written in HTML may cause the recipient's mail client to transmit the recipient's address, or any other unique key, to the spammer's Web site. Likewise, spammers sometimes operate Web pages which purport to remove submitted addresses from spam lists. In several cases, these have been found to subscribe the entered addresses to receive more spam.

Internet users and system administrators have deployed a vast array of techniques to block, filter, or otherwise banish spam from users' mailboxes. Almost all internet service providers forbid the use of their services to send spam or to operate spam-support services. Both commercial firms and volunteers run subscriber services dedicated to blocking or filtering spam, such as AppRiver, Brightmail, Postini, and the various DNSBLs.

A common practice of spammers is to create accounts on free webmail services, such as Hotmail, to send spam or to receive e-mailed responses from potential customers. Because of the amount of mail sent by spammers, they require several e-mail accounts, and use web bots to automate the creation of these accounts. In an effort to cut down on this abuse, many of these services have adopted a system called the captcha: users attempting to create a new account are presented with a graphic of a word, which uses a strange font, on a difficult to read background. Humans are able to read these graphics, and are required to enter the word to complete the application for a new account, while computers are unable to get accurate readings of the words using standard OCR techniques. Blind users of captchas typically get an audio sample. Spammers have, however, found a means of circumventing this measure. Reportedly, they have set up sites offering free pornography: to get access to the site, a user displays a graphic from one of these webmail sites, and must enter the word. Once the bot has successfully created the account, the user gains access to the pornographic material.

Early on, spammers discovered that if they sent large quantities of spam directly from their ISP accounts, recipients would complain and ISPs would shut their accounts down. Thus, one of the basic techniques of sending spam has become to send it from someone else's computer and network connection. By doing this, spammers protect themselves in several ways: they hide their tracks, get others' systems to do most of the work of delivering messages, and direct the efforts of investigators towards the other systems rather than the spammers themselves. The increasing broadband usage gave rise to a great number of computers that are online as long as they are turned on, and whose owners do not always take steps to protect them from malware. A botnet consisting of several hundred compromised machines can effortlessly churn out millions of messages per day. This also complicates the tracing of spammers.

In the 1990s, the most common way spammers did this was to use open mail relays. An open relay is an MTA, or mail server, which is configured to pass along messages sent to it from any location, to any recipient. In the original SMTP mail architecture, this was the default behavior: a user could send mail to practically any mail server, which would pass it along towards the intended recipient's mail server. The standard was written in an era before spamming when there were few hosts on the internet, and those on the internet abided by a certain level of conduct.

While this cooperative, open approach was useful in ensuring that mail was delivered, it was vulnerable to abuse by spammers – and abused it soon was. Spammers could forward batches of spam through open relays, leaving the job of delivering the messages up to the relays. In response, mail system administrators concerned about spam began to demand that other mail operators configure MTAs to cease being open relays. The first DNSBLs, such as MAPS RBL and the now-defunct ORBS, aimed chiefly at allowing mail sites to refuse mail from known open relays.

Within a few years, open relays became rare and spammers resorted to other tactics, most prominently the use of open proxies. A proxy is a network service for making indirect connections to other network services. The client connects to the proxy and instructs it to connect to a server. The server perceives an incoming connection from the proxy, not the original client. Proxies have many purposes, including Web-page caching, protection of privacy, filtering of Web content, and selectively bypassing firewalls. An open proxy is one which will create connections for any client to any server, without authentication. Like open relays, open proxies were once relatively common, as many administrators did not see a need to restrict access to them. A spammer can direct an open proxy to connect to a mail server, and send spam through it. The mail server logs a connection from the proxy – not the spammer's own computer. This provides an even greater degree of concealment for the spammer than an open relay, since most relays log the client address in the headers of messages they pass. Open proxies have also been used to conceal the sources of attacks against other services besides mail, such as Web sites or IRC servers.

In 2003, spam investigators saw a radical change in the way spammers sent spam. Rather than searching the global network for exploitable services such as open relays and proxies, spammers began creating "services" of their own. By commissioning computer viruses designed to deploy proxies and other spam-sending tools, spammers could harness hundreds of thousands of end-user computers. Most of the major Windows e-mail viruses of 2003, including the Sobig and Mimail virus families, functioned as spammer viruses: viruses designed expressly to make infected computers available as spamming tools. Besides sending spam, spammer viruses serve spammers in other ways. Beginning in July 2003, spammers started using some of these same viruses to perpetrate distributed denial-of-service (DDoS) attacks upon DNSBLs and other anti-spam resources. Although this was by no means the first time that illegal attacks have been used against anti-spam sites, it was perhaps the first wave of effective attacks. In August of that year, engineering company Osirusoft ceased providing DNSBL mirrors of the SPEWS and other blocklists, after several days of unceasing attack from virus-infected hosts. The very next month, DNSBL operator Monkeys.com succumbed to the attacks as well. Other DNSBL operators, such as Spamhaus, have deployed global mirroring and other anti-DDoS methods to resist these attacks.

Many spam-filtering techniques work by searching for patterns in the headers or bodies of messages. HTML-based e-mail gives the spammer more tools to obfuscate text. Inserting HTML comments between letters can foil some filters, as can including text made invisible by setting the font color to white on a white background, or shrinking the font size to the smallest fine print. Another common ploy involves presenting the text as an image, which is either sent along or loaded from a remote server. This can be foiled by not permitting an e-mail-program to load images.

As Bayesian filtering has become popular as a spam-filtering technique, spammers have started using methods to weaken it. To a rough approximation, Bayesian filters rely on word probabilities. If a message contains many words which are only used in spam, and few which are never used in spam, it is likely to be spam. To weaken Bayesian filters, some spammers now include lines of irrelevant, random words alongside the sales pitch. A variant on this tactic may be borrowed from the Usenet abuser known as "Hipcrime" – to include passages from books taken from Project Gutenberg, or nonsense sentences generated with "dissociated press" algorithms. Randomly generated phrases can create spamoetry (spam poetry) or spam art.

A number of other online activities and business practices are considered by anti-spam activists to be connected to spamming. These are sometimes termed spam-support services: business services, other than the actual sending of spam itself, which permit the spammer to continue operating. Some internet hosting firms advertise bulk-friendly or bulletproof hosting. This means that, unlike most ISPs, they will not terminate a customer for spamming. These hosting firms operate as clients of larger ISPs, and many have eventually been taken offline by these larger ISPs as a result of complaints regarding spam activity. Thus, while a firm may advertise bulletproof hosting, it is ultimately unable to deliver without the connivance of its upstream ISP. However, some spammers have managed to get what is called a pink contract – a contract with the ISP that allows them to spam without being disconnected.

A few companies produce spamware, or software designed for spammers. Spamware varies widely, but may include the ability to import thousands of addresses, to generate random addresses, to insert fraudulent headers into messages, to use dozens or hundreds of mail servers simultaneously, and to make use of open relays. The sale of spamware is illegal in eight U.S. states. So-called millions CDs are commonly advertised in spam. These are CD-ROMs purportedly containing lists of e-mail addresses, for use in sending spam to these addresses.

Messaging Spam

Messaging spam, sometimes called SPIM, is a type of spam where the target is instant messaging services. The increase in messaging spam may be motivated by its rise in popularity as well as the many steps to crack down on spamming since the late 1990s. Instant messaging (IM) systems, such as Yahoo! Messenger, AIM, MSN Messenger and ICQ, are popular targets for spammers. Many IM systems offer a directory of users, including demographic information such as age and sex. Advertisers can gather this information, sign on to the system, and send unsolicited messages.

Newsgroup Spam

Newsgroup spam is a type of spam where the targets are Usenet newsgroups. Spamming of Usenet newsgroups actually pre-dates e-mail spam. The first widely recognised Usenet spam was posted on January 18, 1994 by Clarence L. Thomas IV, a sysadmin at Andrews University. Entitled "Global Alert for All: Jesus is Coming Soon", it was a fundamentalist religious tract claiming that "this world's history is coming to a climax." The newsgroup posting bot Serdar Argic also appeared in early 1994, posting tens of thousands of messages to various newsgroups, consisting of identical copies of a political screed relating to the Armenian Genocide.

The first commercial Usenet spam, and the one which is often claimed to be the first Usenet spam of any sort, was an advertisement for legal services entitled "Green Card Lottery—Final One?". It was posted in April 1994 by Arizona lawyers Laurence Canter and Martha Siegel, and hawked legal representation for United States immigrants seeking papers. Usenet convention defines spamming as excessive multiple posting, that is, the repeated posting of a message (or substantially similar messages). During the early 1990s there was substantial controversy among Usenet system administrators (news admins) over the use of cancel messages to control spam. A cancel message is a directive to news servers to delete a posting, causing it to be inaccessible to those who might read it. Some regarded this as a bad precedent, leaning towards censorship, while others considered it a proper use of the available tools to control the growing spam problem.

A culture of neutrality towards content precluded defining spam on the basis of advertisement or commercial solicitations. The word "spam" was usually taken to mean excessive multiple posting (EMP), and other neologisms were coined for other abuses — such as "velveeta" (from the processed cheese product) for excessive cross-posting. A subset of spam was deemed cancellable spam, for which it is considered justified to issue third-party cancel messages. In the late 1990s, spam became used as a means of vandalising newsgroups, with malicious users committing acts of sporgery to make targeted newsgroups all but unreadable without heavily filtering.

Spamdexing

Spamdexing or search engine spamming is the practice of deliberately and dishonestly manipulating search engines to increase the chance of a website or page being placed close to the beginning of search engine results, or to influence the category to which the page is assigned in a dishonest manner. Many designers of web pages try to get a good ranking in search engines and design their pages accordingly.

Spamdexing .practices are dishonest and mislead search and indexing programs to give a page a ranking it does not deserve. "White hat" techniques for making a website indexable by search engines, without misleading the indexation process, are known as search engine optimisation (SEO). SEO techniques do not involve deceit.Search engine spammers, on the contrary, are generally aware that the content that they promote is not very useful or relevant to the ordinary internet surfer. Search engines use a variety of algorithms to determine relevancy ranking. Some of these include determining whether the search term appears in the META keywords tag, others whether the search term appears in the body text of a web page. A variety of techniques are used to spamdex. Many search engines check for instances of spamdexing and will remove suspect pages from their indexes.

The rise of spamdexing in the mid-1990s made the leading search engines of the time less useful, and the success of Google at both producing better search results and combating keyword spamming, through its reputation-based PageRank link analysis system, helped it become the dominant search site late in the decade, where it remains. While it has not been rendered useless by spamdexing, Google has not been immune to more sophisticated methods either. Google bombing is another form of web vandalism, which involves creating pages that directly affect the rank of other sites.

Spamware

Spamware is the software used by people in the spam business. The creators of these software packages prefer to call them e-mail marketing packages and there are numerous packages available on the internet. It should be mentioned that the creators of many of these applications also offer "Enterprise Editions" in order for the spammer to operate in a continuous, expeditious mode. Many spammers run fire-and-forget operations where they send out as much spam as possible to a great number of users, then they close down the operation and move to another ISP or open relay. Plug-ins and gateways are available (at a price) for many applications that provide extra functionality to spamware, e.g. gateways that automatically convert e-mail messages (SMTP) to different formats such as MAPI (Mail/Messaging Applications Programming Interface) and SMS (Short Message Service) text messages.

There are some companies that sell spamware as well as conventional software like anti-virus packages and operating systems. What is remarkable is the fact that these companies proudly advertise the seedy features of their spamware products such as the ability to use open relays, forge the header message ID, add a fake sender in the header, and include bogus received from/by lines that are intended to mask the spammer's identity.

- *E-mail Harvester/Extractor*: E-mail Harvester software is designed to extract e-mail addresses from internet sources. An atomic e-mail hunter supports mult-thread page loading and filters can be used to limit the scanning depth i.e. the dept that the extractor will travel within a web site – usually measured in levels. Other extractors will allow e-mail extraction using keywords, which is used to target audiences. It works by entering the topic into a text box. The program then searches for e-mail addresses from the top ranked pages retrieved from popular search engines. This keyword search can be a powerful tool for spammers who want to target spam to specific groups of individuals.

– *Desktop Server Software:* The desktop server software package converts a home user's PC into an e-mail server with the primary purpose of sending bulk e-mail. This software package contains options that exports and imports large lists and has the ability to personalise spam, which means it can associate the recipient's actual name with the e-mail address. The spam message would then appear as if the e-mail was specifically written for the recipient with the aim of adding credibility to the message. It is known that people are more likely to read email that begins with a reference to their name.

– *E-mail List Verifier*: The E-mail List Verifier application checks the validity of e-mail addresses. This is another powerful tool in the spammer's arsenal as it substantially cleans a mail list database that has been polluted by anti-spam devices, such as spider traps. The verifier software checks the syntax of the e-mail addresses and flags incorrectly formatted addresses such as spambait!@aol.com. The software also checks the availability of the address domain, such as yahoo.com and hotmail.com, and flags non-existent domain. Some verifiers may go another step and check the validity of the e-mail addresses by establishing an SMTP connection with the mail server and testing the address there. This is of course very time consuming and the spammer has the option to skip this process.

- *E-mail List Manager*: The List Manager has features that remove duplicates, count e-mail addresses, extract email addresses and names from lists, verify and validate lists, sort list files and filter lists based on specific words.
- *Targeting Software*: There are programs developed for bulk e-mailers that are intended to target particular audiences. Targeting software allows spammers to collect e-mail addresses within a specific marketing area and send spam messages to that locality or group of individuals.

Strategies of Spamming

Spammer tactics are diverse so in this section there is a comprehensive examination of the various methods used by spammers to obtain e-mail addresses and send spam. Thereis also a very interesting section on why some spammers make every effort to detract the attention of those users and organisations that are more likely to react negatively to their spam.

Dictionary attack

During a five-month period in late 2002 and early 2003, spammers conducted a massive dictionary attack to obtain the e-mail addresses of millions of users on the mail servers of Hotmail and MSN. In a dictionary attack, the spammer uses software to create every conceivable variation of a person's name. They would use common first names and common last names and combine them.

Spambots

A spambot is a piece of software, usually written in C for speed and portability, with the primary purpose to crawl through the internet looking for e-mail addresses. They are also called spiders, deviant web crawlers, harvesters or robots. The spambot needs a starting URL from which it collects e-mail addresses and other URLs. The addresses are then stored in a database for use in the creation of a spam list, and the URLs are stored as a source for other web links to crawl in order to locate more e-mail addresses.

Bandwidth Theft

With the popularity of wireless networks and the prevalence of unsecured wireless access points, spammers are now targeting these networks to send out bulk e-mail. The modus operandi involves the spammer driving around hotspot locations and when an unsecured access point is found, it is used to send out a deluge of spam. It is a stealth operation, with the spammer vacating the area before the system administrators finds out that the network is an unwitting source of spam.

Bypassing Filters

Content filters are designed to look for occurrences of certain words in an e-mail message and the spammers' task is to get these words to the recipient without having the e-mail flagged as spam. Spammers bypass filters using one or more of the following methods. The image e-mail is an e-mail that contains nothing but an image or a link to an image. All of the words that a spam filter would generally catch are imbedded in the image. The filter could be redesigned to stop all e-mails with images, but this would also prevent legitimate e-mails with images.

Modem Hijacking

Modem Hijackings occur when unauthorised software uses a computer to dial up to a website that bills the phone owner with exorbitant call charges. This software can be installed unknowingly by opening up a spam attachment or as the result of a rogue popup advertisement. If fallen prey to such a scam, the call charges should be disputed with the phone company. Software is also available that prevents modem hijacking.

Identity Theft

In early 2003, users of America Online received e-mails requesting their passwords and other personal information. Once this type of information is compromised, a person's stolen identity could be used to make credit-card purchases and commit other fraudulentdealings. Many users of other online providers have experienced the same spam scam. It should be noted that credit card firms and ISPs would never ask their customers to reveal passwords or any other personal information in such a manner. These e-mails should not be responded to, but reported to the relevant authorities.

Scam websites

Another spam scam going around at the moment are e-mails that suggest that the recipient could find out what gossip was posted about them on a particular web site. There is a web site called word-of-mouth.org, registered in the Philippines, which invites users to write gossip about other people whose e-mail address they have to include. The company then contacts the owner of this e-mail address with instructions on how to view the gossip, for a fee. Deleting the e-mail is the solution for this scam.

Computer viruses

Unfortunately, there are numerous e-mails rooming the internet that contain viruses with varying degrees of destructive powers. E-mail from unknown users should not be opened. However, there are viruses that can steal e-mail addresses in personal address books stored on computers, so it may appear that the e-mail is coming from someone that is known to the recipient. This is the trademark of viruses known as worms. The only solution to this problem is to make sure that the virus definition files are up-to-date and to confirm any attachment from a sender before opening it up. If in any doubt, do not open attachments and especially do not open files that end with the following extensions: VBS, PIF, SCR and BAT.

Credit/Debt Repair

This spam scam advertises debt or credit card repair. For a fee, companies like ClearCredit.com and GetCleanCredit.com will offer to rectify any credit problems that a person may be experiencing. After providing their credit card numbers, the consumer finds that these companies charged their cards for unauthorised services, often ending up in more debt than before receiving the spam message. Deleting the e-mail is the easy solution for this type of scam.

SPOOFING

A spoofing attack is like a con game: the attacker sets up a false but convincing world around the victim. The victim does something that would be appropriate if the false world were real. Unfortunately, activities that seem reasonable in the false world may have disastrous effects in the real world. Spoofing attacks are possible in the physical world as well as the electronic one. For example, there have been several incidents in which criminals set up bogus automated-teller machines, typically in the public areas of shopping malls. The machines would accept ATM cards and ask the person to enter their PIN code. Once the machine had the victim's PIN, it could either eat the card or "malfunction" and return the card. In either case, the criminals had enough information to copy the victim's card and use the duplicate. In these attacks, people were fooled by the context they saw: the location of the machines, their size and weight, the way they were decorated, and the appearance of their electronic displays.

To appreciate the range and severity of possible spoofing attacks, we must look more deeply into two parts of the definition of spoofing: security-relevant decisions and context. By security-relevant decision, we mean any decision a person makes that might lead to undesirable results such as a breach of privacy or unauthorised tampering with data. Deciding to divulge sensitive information, for example by typing in a password or account number, is one example of a security-relevant decision. Choosing to accept a downloaded document is a security-relevant decision, since in many cases a downloaded document is capable of containing malicious elements that harm the person receiving the document. Even the decision to accept the accuracy of information displayed by your computer can be security-relevant.

ARP spoofing

A computer connected to an IP/Ethernet LAN has two addresses. One is the address of the network card, called the MAC address. The MAC, in theory, is a globally unique and unchangeable address which is stored on the network card itself. MAC addresses are necessary so that the Ethernet protocol can send data back and forth, independent of whatever application protocols are used on top of it. Ethernet builds "frames" of data, consisting of 1500 byte blocks. Each frame has an ethernet header, containing the MAC address of the source and the destination computer. The second address is the IP address. IP is a protocol used by applications, independent of whatever network technology operates underneath it.

Each computer on a network must have a unique IP address to communicate. IP addresses are virtual and are assigned via software. IP and Ethernet must work together. IP communicates by constructing "packets" which are similar to frames, but have a different structure. These packets cannot be delivered without the network layer. In our case they are delivered by Ethernet, which splits the packets into frames, adds an Ethernet header for delivery, and sends them down the cable to the switch. The switch then decides which port to send the frame to, by comparing the destination address of the frame to an internal table which maps port numbers to MAC addresses.

When an Ethernet frame is constructed, it must be built from an IP packet. However, at the time of construction, Ethernet has no idea what the MAC address of the destination machine is, which it needs to create an Ethernet header. The only information it has available is the destination IP from the packet's header. There must be a way for the Ethernet protocol to find the MAC address of the destination machine, given a destination IP. This is where ARP, the Address Resolution Protocol, comes in. ARP operates by sending out "ARP request" packets. An ARP request asks the question, "Is your IP address x.x.x.x? If so, send your MAC back to me." These packets are broadcast to all computers on the LAN, even on a switched network. Each computer examines the ARP request, checks if it is currently assigned the specified IP, and sends an ARP reply containing its MAC address.To minimise the number of ARP packets being broadcast, operating systems keep a cache of ARP replies. When a computer receives an ARP reply, it will update its ARP cache with the new IP/MAC association. As ARP is a stateless protocol, most operating systems will update their cache if a reply is received, regardless of whether they have sent out an actual request.

ARP spoofing involves constructing forged ARP request and reply packets. By sending forged ARP replies, a target computer could be convinced to send frames destined for computer A to instead go to computer B. When done properly, computer A will have no idea that this redirection took place. The process of updating a target computer's ARP cache with a forged entry is referred to as "poisoning". ARP spoofing is a technique used to attack an Ethernet network which may allow an attacker to sniff data frames on a switched local area network (LAN) or stop the traffic altogether.

The principle of ARP spoofing is to send fake, or 'spoofed', ARP messages to an Ethernet LAN. These frames contain false MAC addresses, confusing network devices, such as network switches. As a result frames intended for one machine can be mistakenly sent to another or an unreachable host. ARP spoofing can also be used in a man-in-the-middle attack in which all traffic is forwarded through a host with the use of ARP spoofing and analysed for passwords and other information. Using static ARP records can be effective methods of defence against ARP spoofing attacks. There are also certain tools available that watch the local ARP cache and report to the administrator if anything unusual happens.

Spoofing Attacks

Sniffing

Switches determine which frames go to which ports by comparing the destination MAC on an frame against a table. This table contains a list of ports and the attached MAC address. The table is built when the switch is powered on, by examining the source MAC from the first frame transmitted on each port. Network cards can enter a state called "promiscuous mode" where they are allowed to examine frames that are destined for MAC addresses other than their own. On switched networks this is not a concern, because the switch routes frames based on the table described above. This prevents sniffing of other people's frames.

However, using ARP spoofing, there are several ways that sniffing can be performed on a switched network. A "man-in-the-middle" attack is one of these. When a MiM is performed, a malicious user inserts his computer between the communications path of two target computers. Sniffing can then be performed. The malicious computer will forward frames between the two target computers so communications are not interrupted. The attack is performed as follows (where X is the attacking computer, and T1 and T2 are targets):

- X poisons the ARP cache of T1 and T2.
- T1 associates T2's IP with X's MAC.
- T2 associates T1's IP with X's MAC.
- All of T1 and T2's IP traffic will then go to X first, instead of directly to each other.

This is extremely potent when we consider that not only can computers be poisoned, but routers/gateways as well. All internet traffic for a host could be intercepted with this method by performing a MiM on a target computer and the LAN's router. Another method of sniffing on a switched network is MAC flooding. By sending spoofed ARP replies to a switch at an extremely rapid rate, the switch's port/MAC table will overflow. Results vary by brand, but some switches will revert to broadcast mode at this point. Sniffing can then be performed.

DOS

Updating ARP caches with non-existent MAC addresses will cause frames to be dropped. These could be sent out in a sweeping fashion to all clients on the network in order to cause a Denial of Service attack. This is also a side effect of post-MiM attacks, since targeted computers will continue to send frames to the attacker's MAC address even after they remove themselves from the communication path. To perform a clean MiM attack, the target computers would have to have the original ARP entries restored by the attacking computer.

Hijacking

Connection hijacking allows an attacker to take control of a connection between two computers, using methods similar to the MiM attack. This transfer of control can result in any type of session being transferred. For example, an attacker could take control of a telnet session after a target computer has logged in to a remote computer as administrator.

Cloning

MAC addresses were intended to be globally-unique identifiers for each network interface produced. They were to be burned into the ROM of each interface, and not be changed. Today, however, MAC addresses are easily changed. Linux users can even change their MAC without spoofing software, using a single parameter to "ifconfig", the interface configuration program for the OS. An attacker could DoS a target computer, then assign themselves the IP and MAC of the target computer, receiving all frames intended for the target.

Spoofing Tools

ARPoison

ARPoison is a command-line tool for UNIX which creates spoofed ARP packets. Users can specify the source and destination IP/MAC addresses.

Ettercap

Ettercap is a powerful program UNIX program employing a text-mode GUI, easy enough to be used by "script kiddies". All operations are automated, and the target computers are chosen from a scrollable list of hosts detected on the LAN. Ettercap can perform four methods of sniffing: IP, MAC, ARP, and Public ARP. It also automates the following procedures:

- Injecting characters into connections.
- Sniffing encrypted SSH sessions.
- Password collection.
- OS fingerprinting.
- Connection killing.

Parasite

Parasite is a daemon which watches a LAN for ARP requests, and automatically sends spoofed ARP replies. This places the attacking computer as the MiM for any computer that broadcasts and ARP request. Eventually, this results in a LAN-wide MiM attack and all data on the switch can be sniffed. Parasite does not do a proper clean-up when stopped. This results in a DoS of all poisoned computers because their ARP caches are pointing to a MAC address that is no longer forwarding their frames. Poisoned ARP entries must expire before normal operation can resume.

Web Spoofing

Web spoofing is a kind of electronic con game in which the attacker creates a convincing but false copy of the entire World Wide Web. The false web looks just like the real one: it has all the same pages and links. However, the attacker controls the false web, so that all network traffic between the victim's browser and the web goes through the attacker. Since the attacker can observe or modify any data going from the victim to web servers, as well as controlling all return traffic from web servers to the victim, the attacker has many possibilities. These include surveillance and tampering.

– *Surveillance*: The attacker can passively watch the traffic, recording which pages the victim visits and the contents of those pages. When the victim fills out a form, the entered data is transmitted to a web server, so the attacker can record that too, along with the response sent back by the server. Since most on-line commerce is done via forms, this means the attacker can observe any account numbers or passwords the victim enters. The attacker can carry out surveillance even if the victim has a "secure" connection to the server, that is, even if the victim's browser shows the secure-connection icon.

– *Tampering*: The attacker is also free to modify any of the data traveling in either direction between the victim and the web. The attacker can modify form data submitted by the victim. For example, if the victim is ordering a product on-line, the attacker can change the product number, the quantity, or the ship-to address.

The attacker can also modify the data returned by a web server, for example by inserting misleading or offensive material in order to trick the victim or to cause antagonism between the victim and the server. You may think it is difficult for the attacker to spoof the entire web, but it is not. The attacker need not store the entire contents of the web. The whole web is available on-line; the attacker's server can just fetch a page from the real web when it needs to provide a copy of the page on the false web. The key to this attack is for the attacker's web server to sit between the victim and the rest of the web. This kind of arrangement is called a "man in the middle attack" in the security literature. The attacker's first trick is to rewrite all of the URLs on some web page so that they point to the attacker's server rather than to some real server. Assuming the attacker's server is on the machine www.attacker.org, the attacker rewrites a URL by adding http://www.attacker.org to the front of the URL.

Once the attacker's server has fetched the real document needed to satisfy the request, the attacker rewrites all of the URLs in the document into the same special form by splicing http://www.attacker.org/ onto the front. Then the attacker's server provides the rewritten page to the victim's browser. Since all of the URLs in the rewritten page now pcint to www.attacker.org, if the victim follows a link on the new page, the page will again be fetched through the attacker's server. The victim remains trapped in the attacker's false web, and can follow links forever without leaving it.

If the victim fills out a form on a page in a false web, the result appears to be handled properly. Spoofing of forms works naturally because forms are integrated closely into the basic web protocols: form submissions are encoded in web requests and the replies are ordinary HTML. Since any URL can be spoofed, forms can also be spoofed. When the victim submits a form, the submitted data goes to the attacker's server. The attacker's server can observe and even modify the submitted data, doing whatever malicious editing desired, before passing it on to the real server. The attacker's server can also modify the data returned in response to the form submission.

One distressing property of this attack is that it works even when the victim requests a page via a "secure" connection. If the victim does a "secure" web access (a web access using the Secure Sockets Layer) in a false web, everything will appear normal: the page will be delivered, and the secure connection indicator (usually an image of a lock or key) will be turned on. The victim's browser says it has a secure connection because it does have one. Unfortunately the secure connection is to www.attacker.org and not to the place the victim thinks it is. The victim's browser thinks everything is fine: it was told to access a URL at www.attacker.org so it made a secure connection to www.attacker.org. The secure-connection indicator only gives the victim a false sense of security.

To start an attack, the attacker must somehow lure the victim into the attacker's false web. There are several ways to do this. An attacker could put a link to a false web onto a popular web page. If the victim is using web-enabled email, the attacker could email the victim a pointer to a false web, or even the contents of a page in a false web. Finally, the attacker could trick a web search engine into indexing part of a false web

The attack as described thus far is fairly effective, but it is not perfect. There is still some remaining context that can give the victim clues that the attack is going on. However, it is possible for the attacker to eliminate virtually all of the remaining clues of the attack's existence. Such evidence is not too hard to eliminate because browsers are very customisable. The ability of a web page to control browser behavior is often desirable, but when the page is hostile it can be dangerous.

The status line is a single line of text at the bottom of the browser window that displays various messages, typically about the status of pending web transfers. The attack as described so far leaves two kinds of evidence on the status line. First, when the mouse is held over a web link, the status line displays the URL the link points to. Thus, the victim might notice that a URL has been rewritten. Second, when a page is being fetched, the status line briefly displays the name of the server being contacted. Thus, the victim might notice that www.attacker.org is displayed when some other name was expected. The attacker can cover up both of these cues by adding a JavaScript program to every rewritten page. Since JavaScript programs can write to the status line, and since it is possible to bind JavaScript actions to the relevant events, the attacker can arrange things so that the status line participates in the con game, always showing the victim what would have been on the status line in the real web. This makes the spoofed context even more convincing.

The browser's location line displays the URL of the page currently being shown. The victim can also type a URL into the location line, sending the browser to that URL. The attack as described so far causes a rewritten URL to appear in the location line, giving the victim a possible indication that an attack is in progress.m This clue can be hidden using JavaScript. A JavaScript program can hide the real location line and replace it by a fake location line that looks right and is in the expected place. The fake location line can show the URL the victim expects to see. The fake location line can also accept keyboard input, allowing the victim to type in URLs normally. The JavaScript program can rewrite typed-in URLs before they are accessed.

Popular browsers offer a menu item that allows the user to examine the HTML source for the currently displayed page. A user could possibly look for rewritten URLs in the HTML source, and could therefore spot the attack. The attack can prevent this by using JavaScript to hide the browser's menu bar, replacing it with a menu bar that looks just like the original. If the user chose "view document source" from the spoofed menu bar, the attacker would open a new window to display the original (non-rewritten) HTML source. A related clue is available if the victim chooses the browser's "view document information" menu item. This will display information including the document's URL. As above, this clue can be spoofed by replacing the browser's menu bar. This leaves no remaining visible clues to give away the attack.

Some people have suggested that finding and punishing the attacker can deter this attack. It is true that the attacker's server must reveal its location in order to carry out the attack, and that evidence of that location will almost certainly be available after an attack is detected. Unfortunately, this will not help much in practice because attackers will break into the machine of some innocent person and launch the attack there. Stolen machines will be used in these attacks for the same reason most bank robbers make their getaways in stolen cars.

Defending Web Spoofing

Web spoofing is a dangerous and nearly undetectable security attack that can be carried out on today's internet. Fortunately there are some protective measures you can take. In the short run, the best defense is to follow a three-part strategy:

1. disable JavaScript in your browser so the attacker will be unable to hide the evidence of the attack;
2. make sure your browser's location line is always visible;
3. pay attention to the URLs displayed on your browser's location line, making sure they always point to the server you think you're connected to.

This strategy will significantly lower the risk of attack, though you could still be victimised if you are not conscientious about watching the location line. At present, JavaScript, ActiveX, and Java all tend to facilitate spoofing and other security attacks, so we recommend that you disable them. Doing so will cause you to lose some useful functionality, but you can recoup much of this loss by selectively turning on these features when you visit a trusted site that requires them.

Cyber Stalking

Cyber stalking is the use of the internet, e-mail, or other electronic communications devices to stalk another person. Stalking generally involves harassing or threatening behaviour that an individual engages in repeatedly, such as following a person, appearing at a person's home or place of business, making harassing phone calls, leaving written messages or objects, or vandalising a person's property. Most stalking laws require that the perpetrator make a credible threat of violence against the victim; others include threats against the victim's immediate family; and still others require only that the alleged stalker's course of conduct constitute an implied threat. While some conduct involving annoying or menacing behaviour might fall short of illegal stalking, such behaviour may be a prelude to stalking and violence and should be treated seriously.

Cyber stalking is analogous to traditional forms of stalking in that it incorporates persistent behaviours that instill apprehension and fear. However, because by definition cyber stalking takes place in a 'virtual' environment, it draws our attention to what is distinct about the world of the internet and the way it incorporates dimensions never envisaged by those seeking to control behaviour though legislation. Cyber stalking thus entails the same general characteristics as traditional stalking, but in being transposed into the virtual environment it is fundamentally transformed. The nature of this transformation is dependent upon what particular aspects of the internet are exploited. The internet is used by both those with an interest in efficient exercises of "traditional" criminality as well as those attuned to the possibilities of altogether new forms of criminality. In both instances, we need to understand what the internet actually 'is' if we wish to determine the potential for criminality it entails. At present, our attempts to protect the wider community from cyber crimes are hindered by a failure on the part of policy makers to appreciate that the internet offers access to domains beyond the reach of traditional legislative frameworks. This means that before understanding the nature of cyber stalking, we need to first understand the nature of the internet.

When we understand the internet as a composite medium potentially incorporating three quite different types of data exchange interactions, the problematic nature of internet-based crimes quickly becomes apparent. Cyber crimes can in some instances closely resemble real world crimes but in other instances are so virtual that their connection with the real world is tenuous and constantly shifting. Cyber stalking provides an illuminating example of what it means to be faced with fertile new ground in which crime can flourish untroubled by effective surveillance and control. The extent to which cyber stalking can be routinely regulated and responded to by the criminal justice system depends upon the extent to which it occurs as an articulation of the first of the three highlighted types of interaction. Control of the second type of interaction may prove to be achievable via technological 'fixes' of one sort or another, but exploitation of the third type of interaction takes us into entirely foreign territory where "the old ways no longer hold good".

The person to person or organisation to organisation communications identified as the first type of exchange, are conceptually not so very different from old-fashioned postal communications and can in all likelihood be regulated by extensions to current legislative initiatives, as has indeed been undertaken in the United States. Email correspondence may be kept as "evidence" of a concerning act and current stalking legislation should theoretically allow for e-mail to be considered a threatening communication. The more predatory second type of exchange may be highly problematic but it is not unreasonable to expect a technical fix that renders internet users less exposed to the Windows "backdoor". Conceptually, this second form of interaction simply represents a new expression of the "old crime" of misappropriation. Whilst apprehension of the perpetrator of such a crime may or may not prove to be possible, defining such activities as "illegal" would not be difficult.

The third type of data exchange mechanism however is quite different from the other two types and presents serious challenges to both pre-internet conceptions of social interactions based upon data exchanges, and any attempts to regulate such interactions. In a further "twist", this third type of interaction is increasingly opening up possibilities for the evolution of new forms of the other two types of data exchanges.

Internet developments such as NAPSTER, Freenet and Gnutella permit data exchanges in such a way that they can no longer be readily understood in terms of concepts that pre-date the internet and are increasingly resistant to notions of control that pre-date the internet. Users of networks such as Freenet become members of virtual communities whose internal communications are extraordinarily difficult if not impossible to either monitor or regulate. In the future, this avenue for communication might well come to include highly invasive and predatory email type communications that would be essentially immune to any attempts at control. In examining this third form of interaction, the internet needs to be recognised as a new medium of communication rather than the "latest version" of the old mediums. In discussing the internet we are not discussing traditional criminal contexts. Instead, we are faced with substantial challenges to legislative and regulatory controls that rely upon clearly definable jurisdictional contexts and clearly definable behaviours.

Even assuming it is possible to resolve these new jurisdictional problems it is far from clear that anything could be done to actually "bring the cyber stalker to justice". At least as far as the internet is concerned, the "stalker" is after all nothing more than a digital address. While such addresses may be traced, they may also be continually hidden, shifted, and altered. Whilst it can be argued that some cyber crimes are no different from real world crimes in as much as they reflect the same range of offensive and dangerous behaviours, it also needs to be acknowledged that the internet can magnify, distort and ignore the attributes of the real world in ways we urgently need to address. The first step in effectively responding to internet based crime in general and cyber stalking in particular, is to ensure our understanding of the internet is derived from a realistic appreciation of the nature of the new technologies themselves rather than being rooted in a pre-internet conception of information exchange mechanisms.

Categories of Cyber Stalking

Cyber stalking is analogous to traditional forms of stalking in that it incorporates persistent behaviours that instil apprehension and fear. However, with the advent of new technologies, traditional stalking has taken on entirely new forms through mediums such as email and the internet. Thus, it becomes cyber stalking. Increasingly, cyber stalking is gaining the attention of the media and the public as the nature of the crime incorporates elements of new technology and threatening behaviours, which symbolise a new form of threat. Unfortunately, we have absolutely no empirical research upon which to estimate the actual incidence of cyber stalking and, indeed, determining the magnitude of this crime is practically impossible. It has been argued, however, that such incidents may be more common than traditional forms of stalking. This is because the basic apparatus of the internet, including free email and chat rooms, facilitate contact with an immense field of potential victims. For example, "a single user can send the same file to hundreds of people in far less time than it would take to telephone or write them". The manner in which cyber stalking is conducted, however, is dependent upon the particular use of the internet being exploited.

There are three primary ways in which cyber stalking is conducted.

1. *Email stalking*: Direct communication through email.
2. *Internet stalking*: Global communication through the internet.
3. *Computer stalking*: Unauthorised control of another person's computer.

Email Stalking

While the most common forms of stalking in the physical world involve telephoning, sending mail, and actual surveillance, cyber stalking can take many forms. Unsolicited email is one of the most common forms of harassment, including hate, obscene, or threatening mail. Other forms of harassment include sending the victim viruses or high volumes of electronic junk mail. Sending viruses or telemarketing solicitations alone do not constitute stalking. However, if these communications are repetitively sent in a manner which is designed to intimidate, then they may constitute "concerning behaviours" and hence be categorised as stalking.

In many ways, stalking via email represents the closest replication of traditional stalking patterns. Given that the most common forms of stalking behaviour are telephoning and sending mail, the adoption of email by stalkers is not surprising. As a medium, email incorporates the immediacy of a phone call and introduces the degree of separation entailed in a letter. It might be argued that email stalking is actually less invasive than phone calls because the victim can undermine the interaction by deleting, without opening, any suspicious or unsolicited messages. This argument does, however, deny the social meaning of email communication.

As with telephone stalking, email harassment constitutes an uninvited and arguably threatening incursion into private space. As with stalking in the physical world, email stalking can result from an attempt to initiate a relationship, repair a relationship, or threaten and traumatise a person. Interestingly though, those cases which have been prosecuted have tended to fall into the latter category.

Internet Stalking

Stalkers can more comprehensively use the internet in order to slander and endanger their victims. In such cases, the cyber stalking takes on a public, rather than a private, dimension. In one example, a female university lecturer was stalked for some years. Her ex-boyfriend would visit her usual chat sites, and then follow her from site to site, recording where she went. He also posted false information about her in various chat sites, including both those she habited and pornography sites that he visited. Finally, he hunted down and distributed semipornographic photographs of her as a young girl across the net. In another example, a woman was stalked for a period of 6 months. Her harasser posted notes in a chat room that threatened to rape and kill her, and posted doctored pornographic pictures of her on the net together with personal details. What is particularly disturbing about this second form of cyber stalking is that it appears to be the most likely to spill over into "physical space". In these instances, cyber stalking is accompanied by traditional stalking behaviours such as threatening phone calls, vandalism of property, threatening mail, and physical attacks.

In real life, stalkers usually stalk in proximity to their victims—they want the victim to see them and know they are there—they feed on the victim's reaction. On the Net, proximity takes on a new meaning. Obviously, there are important differences between the situation of someone who is regularly within shooting range of her or his stalker and someone who is being stalked from two thousand miles away.While the previous examples can be viewed as offensive and threatening, they can, nevertheless, be viewed as distinct from "traditional" stalking in that they remain in cyber space. While emotional distress is acknowledged in most criminal sanctions, it is not considered as serious as actual physical threat. Thus, while links between stalking, domestic violence, and femicide have been empirically demonstrated "in real life", much cyber stalking remains at the level of inducing emotional distress, fear, and apprehension. However, this is not to say that causing apprehension and fear should not be criminally sanctioned, or that the cyber and the real are somehow inherently or intrinsically disconnected.

Cyber stalking can be simply an electronic precursor to real world behaviours. An example of the blurring lines between cyber and physical stalking involved a Los Angeles security guard whose romantic advances were rejected by a 28- year-old woman. In response, he impersonated her in chat rooms, and, pretending to be her, posted the woman's name, address, and phone number on the internet, claiming that she was looking for men who would provide substance to her rape fantasies.The result of these postings was that the woman was "repeatedly awakened in the middle of the night by men banging on her front door, shouting that they were there to rape her." Similarly, an author was stalked by a publishing company who, among other techniques such as spamming, also placed her name, home address, and home phone number on the web, with an advertisement saying that she "would be available for sex anytime, day or night". Needless to say, she received multiple proposals.

Computer Stalking

In this category of cyber stalking, this defensive strategy is undermined by the stalker. In essence, the stalker exploits the workings of the internet and the Windows operating system in order to assume control over the computer of the targeted victim. It is probably not widely recognised that an individual "Windows based" computer connected to the internet can be identified, and connected to, by another computer connected to the internet. This "connection" is not the "link" via a third party characterising typical internet interactions; rather, it is a computer-to-computer connection allowing the interloper to exercise control over the computer of the target.

At present, a reasonably high degree of computer "savvy" is required to undertake this form of exploitation of the internet and the Windows operating system.

However, and inevitably, instructions on how to use the technologies in this way are available on the internet. It is likely that progressively easier "scripts" for the exercise will be made freely available for anyone so inclined to download. In practice, what this means is that individual computer users have a vastly reduced buffer between themselves and the stalker.

A cyber stalker can communicate directly with their target as soon as the target computer connects in any way to the internet. The stalker can assume control of the victim's computer and the only defensive option for the victim is to disconnect and relinquish their current internet "address". The situation is like discovering that anytime you pick up the phone, a stalker is online and in control of your phone. The only way to avoid the stalker is to disconnect the phone completely, and then reconnect with an entirely new number.

Prevention of Cyber stalking

According to the nature of cyber stalking, the opportunities to intervene are varied. There are three primary ways in which cyber stalking can be countered, all of which will have varying degrees of success. They are: personal protection, technical fixes and legislation.

Personal protection: While many may object that personal protection strategies are an infringement upon people's right to travel freely in cyber space, the fact is that personal prevention is taken on a daily basis in the physical world, and the cyber world is no different. Simple strategies such as not providing personal information to strangers are just as, if not more, applicable in cyber space.People who participate in the cyber world will minimise the likelihood of their being stalked by using techniques such as gender neutral and age neutral names. Personal information should not be recorded on the internet and people should hesitate before filling in electronic forms which request names, age, addresses, together with personal likes and dislikes. Similarly, people can be pro-active before signing on to an ISP provider by researching beforehand on whether there are specific policies prohibiting harassment, abusive behaviours, and cyber stalking.

Technical fixes: It is also important to note that many of the solutions to cyber stalking are likely to come about through technological fixes, rather than personal or legislative intervention. Personal familiarity with the many "filter" programs available now, both in chat rooms and many email services, allow users to block unwanted messages, or messages received from unknown sources. Whilst anonymous remailers and browsers further reduce the likelihood of potential stalkers being able toidentify victims. Most specifically, the third type of stalking described, that carried out through control of a computer, is likely to be easily fixed through a technological "patch" which no longer allows people to access other computers.

Role of law enforcement agencies: Cyber stalking is a relatively new challenge for most law enforcement agencies. Traditional stalking law are existing in most countries. Some law enforcement agencies have trained their personnel on stalking and/or established specialised units to handle stalking cases. Nonetheless, many agencies are still developing the expertise and resources to investigate and prosecute traditional stalking cases; only a handful of agencies throughout the country have focused attention or resources specifically on the cyber stalking problem.

Based on recent informal surveys, it appears that the majority of agencies have not investigated or prosecuted any cyber stalking cases. However, some agencies–

particularly those with units dedicated to stalking or computer crime offenses have large cyber stalking caseloads. For example the he New York Police Department's Computer Investigation and Technology Unit and the Los Angeles District Attorney's Stalking and Threat Assessment Team estimate that 40 and 20 percent of their caseloads, respectively, involve cyber stalking-type cases. The disparity in the activity level among law enforcement agencies can be attributed to a number of factors. First, it appears that the majority of cyber stalking victims do not report the conduct to law enforcement, either because they feel that the conduct has not reached the point of being a criminal offense or that law enforcement will not take them seriously. Second, most law enforcement agencies have not had the training to recognise the serious nature of cyber stalking and to investigate such offenses. Unfortunately, some victims have reported that rather than open an investigation, a law enforcement agency has advised them to come back if the cyber stalkers confront or threaten them offline. In several instances, victims have been told by law enforcement simply to turn off their computers.

Another indication that many law enforcement agencies underestimate the magnitude of the cyber stalking problem is the wide disparity in reported cases in different jurisdictions across the country. For example, one state attorney general's office in a midwestern state indicated that it received approximately one inquiry a week regarding cyber stalking cases and that it is aware of approximately a dozen prosecutions last year alone. In contrast, the state attorney general's offices in neighboring states indicated they have never received an inquiry into this type of behaviour. Although one would generally expect some disparity in differing jurisdictions, the size of the disparity suggests that some law enforcement agencies do not have the training or expertise to recognise the magnitude of the problem in their jurisdictions.

Some law enforcement agencies also have been frustrated by jurisdictional limitations. In many instances, the cyber stalker may be located in a different city or state than the victim making it more difficult for the local authority to investigate the incident. Even if a law enforcement agency is willing to pursue a case across state lines, it may be difficult to obtain assistance from out-of-state agencies when the conduct is limited to harassing e-mail messages and no actual violence has occurred. The lack of adequate statutory authority also can limit law enforcement's response to cyber stalking incidents.

Another complication for law enforcement is the presence of services that provide anonymous communications over the internet. To be sure, anonymity provides important benefits, including protecting the privacy of internet users. Unfortunately, cyber stalkers and other cyber criminals can exploit the anonymity available on the internet to avoid accountability for their conduct.

A growing number of law enforcement agencies are recognising the serious nature and extent of cyber stalking and taking aggressive action to respond. Some larger metropolitan areas have seen numerous incidents of cyber stalking and have specialised units available to investigate and prosecute these cases. Traditional law enforcement techniques for surveillance, investigation, and evidence gathering require modification for use on computer networks and often require the use of unfamiliar legal processes. Law enforcement at all levels must be properly trained to use network investigative techniques and legal process while protecting the privacy of legitimate users of the internet. These techniques are similar to those used in investigating other types of computer crime. Just as a burglar might leave fingerprints at the scene of a crime, a cyber stalker can leave an "electronic trail" on the web that properly trained law enforcement can follow back to the source. Thus, technological proficiency among both investigators and prosecutors is essential.

A critical step in combating cyber stalking is understanding stalking in general. In many instances, cyber stalking is simply another phase in an overall stalking pattern, or it is regular stalking behaviour using new, high-technology tools. Thus, strategies and techniques that have been developed to combat stalking in general often can be adapted to cyber stalking situations. Fortunately, many state law enforcement agencies have begun to focus on stalking, and some have developed special task forces to deal with this problem.

4

Digital Piracy

In a networked digital world, creating, modifying, manipulating, and distributing digital copies of copyrighted content is extremely easy. From a content owner's perspective, digital content is much harder to manage and control compared to physical assets. Similarly, because advances in telecommunications, storage, and software technologies have made monitoring a person's activities while surfing the Web effortless, securing personal information and ensuring privacy pose issues of paramount concern to consumers.

Historically, entertainment content owners have responded to the piracy issue by supporting legislative action that prohibits copyright infringement. The information technology industry and service providers constantly seek new business models to support digital distribution of entertainment content. These emerging business models add yet another dimension of complexity to the piracy and copyright infringement issue, requiring new technologies for content protection and distribution. Recent trends indicate that in the future, content owners may be forced to pursue new distribution models based on consumer preferences.

Using the Internet as a distribution channel and computers as rendering devices is appealing because the associated costs and licensing terms are favorable to both producers and consumers. Somewhat surprisingly, efforts to define, develop, and standardize technologies supporting privacy protection are evolving less rapidly. Privacy protection is often not a core component as enterprises plan and build the architecture of the next generation of digital services. Consequently, current protection schemes for financial institutions, the healthcare industry, and even e-commerce vendors are based predominantly on policy and business or legal agreements rather than on enabling technologies.

Beginning in the early 1990s, concern about piracy of digital goods—in particular, entertainment content—led to the development of digital rights management (DRM) technologies. These technologies dynamically control content throughout its entire life cycle, regulating what can be done with that content and the time frame in which it is accessible. DRM typically encompasses all aspects of content creation, including the definition of associated rights, content distribution and consumption, and the enforcement of authorized rights. It also emphasizes consumer-oriented standard protocols and specifications to facilitate interoperability among content owners, service providers, and device manufacturers.

Recent events indicate that the entertainment industry's position may be softening toward newer content distribution models. Since the late 1990s, the music industry has vigorously battled Internet sites that let users download and copy virtually any song without paying. However, the recent ruling in favor of Morpheus peer-to-peer software, which allows file swapping, appears to be a significant setback to the entertainment industry and is being compared to the landmark decision in 1984 in favor of VCR manufacturers against television content owners.

Apple's launch of an online music store for Macintosh computer users, which is integrated with iTunes 4, is emerging as a promising alternative to free, pirated music. The service includes more than 200,000 songs from the five major music labels that can be downloaded for 99 cents each with virtually no restrictions on how and where the songs can be played, including on portable devices. Downloaded songs can be played an unlimited number of times and burned to a CD.

Songs are downloaded using the MPEG-2 ISO Advanced Audio Coding standard, which provides higher quality fidelity with smaller file sizes than the older MP3 standard that it extends. Apple uses AAC to tap into the DRM technologies rolled into QuickTime 6.2, preventing users from swapping the tracks as easily as MP3 files. Users can transfer the AAC files they purchase on the iTunes Music Service to another computer, but iTunes 4 and other AAC playback software require the original purchaser's ID and password to play the downloaded files. Technology that supports the ability to provide inexpensive, easy-to-access, consumer-friendly models for the purchase and distribution of entertainment content is likely to be adopted, standardized, and widely deployed.

While piracy prevention relies on key technologies, regulations generally mandate consumer privacy protection. The 12th Annual Conference on Computers, Freedom, and Privacy held in April 2002 made it clear that vendors are unlikely to build in privacy protection if there is no incentive for profit, which may account for the current lack of privacy protection applications powered by sophisticated technologies. Protecting consumer privacy thus relies more on policy definition tools and a rules-based authorization engine that enforces access control to sensitive information than on technologies such as encryption, key management, or tamper resistance. The Platform for Privacy Preferences Project, developed by the World Wide Web Consortium as an emerging industry standard, has been a significant factor in efforts to protect consumer privacy in the face of corporate marketing. P3P provides a simple automated way for users to gain more control over the use of personal information on Web sites they visit.

At its most basic level, P3P is a standardized set of multiple-choice questions, covering all the major aspects of a Web site's privacy policies. Taken together, the questions present a clear snapshot of how a site handles personal information about its users. P3P-enabled Web sites make this information available in a standard, machine-readable format. P3P-enabled browsers can "read" this snapshot automatically and compare it to the consumer's own set of privacy preferences. P3P enhances user control by putting privacy policies where users can find them and in a form they can understand. Most importantly, users can act on what they see.

In "Protecting Intellectual Property in Digital Multimedia Networks," Ahmet M. Eskicioglu presents an overview of piracy and privacy issues from a content owner's perspective, summarizing copyright industry losses due to piracy, the technical means of protecting IP in digital form, and some of the remaining obstacles to secure digital content distribution and storage. "Protecting Cryptographic Keys: The Trace-and-Revoke Approach" by Dalit Naor and Moni Naor describes two broadcast encryption methods that protect content by creating a legitimate distribution channel. The authors also provide a method for updating user keys to resecure a compromised network and offer a tracing algorithm that uncovers the compromised key's owner.

In "A Trusted Open Platform," Paul England and colleagues present an interesting perspective on technologies relevant to an extensible, open computing platform as the basis for a broad class of applications including piracy prevention and privacy protection. "Preventing Piracy, Reverse Engineering, and Tampering" by Gleb Naumovich and Nasir Memon focuses on three promising techniques-tamperproofing, obfuscation, and watermarking-for preserving and protecting software data. "Technical Challenges of Protecting Digital Entertainment Content" by C. Brendon S. Traw underscores the limitations of currently available technologies in providing a robust piracy prevention solution.

The finance and healthcare industries currently focus on using access control technologies to enforce consumer privacy protection. While some enterprises have adopted the sophisticated P3P policy specification languages, the technologies to enforce these policies are not yet widely deployed. Policies and agreements continue to play a significant role in consumer privacy protection. In contrast, a richer set of technologies including cryptography, key management, tracing traitors, watermarking, and tamper resistance is currently available to prevent content piracy.

Piracy over the Internet

Widespread piracy over the Internet seriously harms the artists, both the famous and struggling, who create content, as well as the technicians-sound engineers, editors, set designers, game programmers-who produce it. Piracy has serious economic implications reaching far beyond the lost revenue of the stealing itself. Many content providers have resisted embracing digital distribution and online business models in part because of fear that digital piracy will eventually destroy their businesses. The degree to which that assumption is true will form the basis of many public policy decisions.

Virtually every product sold to consumers is vulnerable to theft, which is why retail stores spend money to prevent shoplifting. Content is particularly vulnerable in the digital environment, because an infinite number of perfect copies can be made from just one original and because those copies can be distributed cheaply around the globe using the Internet. Completely eliminating this kind of piracy is impossible. Once one copy of a song or film is created free of copy protection measures, it can multiply like a virus until it is widely available.

Until now, this has been a problem confined mostly to the music and software industries, but with the growth of high-speed Internet connections, virtually every content industry is affected. At the same time, if the content industries are not able to achieve some degree of protection for their intellectual property, there are two likely scenarios. One is a marked decrease in the production of high-quality content. The other possibility is a tighter lockdown of content through encryption and other technologies that greatly restrict consumer uses of content. Reaching an acceptable level of protection, of course, will have costs and inconveniences; the goal should be to place those burdens, to the greatest extent possible, on the pirates themselves rather than on the content or technology industries or law-abiding consumers as a whole.

It is possible to keep piracy to a low and manageable level if two things happen. First, the inconvenience of piracy must increase, including the difficulty in finding and downloading pirated content, and the risk of getting caught and punished for doing so. Second, both public and private measures must be taken to make it easier for consumers to acquire content legally, by paying for the content that they download.

If content piracy is made more difficult and content purchasing is made easier, content providers will be able to maintain viable business models even when competing with illegal free downloads on peer-to-peer networks. Pursuing a public policy agenda that facilitates these two changes will have immense economic impacts as content providers stop resisting the digital revolution and embrace the Internet to sell music, movies, software, and other content directly to consumers. This will move us toward the ultimate goal: an environment in which digitally transmitted content is widely available and the creators of the content are fairly compensated for their efforts.

Many cyber libertarians and other advocates who oppose strong copyright protection for content contend that the protests of providers are merely the next step in a long history of resisting new technologies before embracing those technologies and finding new revenue streams. The classic example of this is the popularisation of the video cassette recorder. Movie studios, afraid that inexpensive home recording would increase piracy and put them out of business, fought fiercely against the production of VCRs, eventually leading to a court decision that a technology with "substantial noninfringing uses" cannot automatically be assumed to be a piracy device.Defeated in the legal arena, the studios ultimately embraced the VCR, creating the multi-billion dollar video rental industry and changing the price schemes on video cassettes. The result was lowered video prices—which popularised the purchase of movies for home viewing.

Digital recording technology and the Internet represent a quantum leap forward in piracy tools. Previous worries about widespread piracy may have proven to be exaggerated, but this time the magnitude of the threat is beyond anything that has come before. There are a number of differences between previous generations of recording technology and the new technologies that make piracy significantly easier today. In the past, analog recording technologies such as audio and video cassettes had a built-in check on widespread piracy: The quality of the recording degenerated significantly with each new generation. If a cassette was purchased at the store and copied on a home stereo, the resulting "first generation" copy was slightly degraded but still quite good. If that first generation copy was used to create another copy, the quality of the second generation copy declined precipitously.

Generally speaking, in both audio and video cassettes, the quality of third-generation copies was so poor that most consumers preferred to pay for a pristine copy than get a degraded copy for free. Moreover, the replication media in some cases were more expensive and time-consuming than buying a legal copy, particularly regarding books. These technological limitations on copying do not exist in the digital world. Each copy of a digital audio or video file is exactly as good as the original from which it was made. Thus, a single high-quality file can begin a copy cycle that grows exponentially, as each subsequent copy generation spawns new generations of copies that are just as good as the original.

Once a consumer has invested in a personal computer and Internet connection, each copy is virtually free. While this is an important step forward in the legitimate distribution of content, it also means that the opportunities for piracy are greater than ever before. In the past, the only way to get a pirated copy of a song or video was to come into physical contact with somebody who already had a highquality copy. Though some pirates set up booths at swap meets and on street corners, in general someone seeking a pirated copy needed to have a personal friend who had already purchased the original. This served as a natural break on piracy, as it was frequently easier to buy a cassette than to seek out somebody who had paid for it and was willing to make a copy for free.

The Internet has changed that forever. Napster and its successors-KaZaA, Morpheus, and other file-copying software-allow anonymous individuals around the globe to connect and obtain files or make them available for copying to anyone in the world. The software itself does not make the copies; the simple act of downloading a file from another computer is the copy mechanism. Rather, these programmes serve as massive, real-time search engines, allowing individuals to search millions of networked computers simultaneously for certain files and connect them for download automatically. Thus, it is no longer necessary to know someone who purchased a factory-produced song or video to get a pirated copy; so long as one person out of the millions on the network has it, it can be found and copied in minutes.

These programmes also make file copying easier by allowing the pirates to remain relatively anonymous; short of a court issued subpoena to an Internet Service Provider (ISP), it is virtually impossible to identify individuals engaged in copying. File Copying Instead of File Swapping One of the biggest misconceptions in the digital copyright debate is the idea that copying that occurs on Napster-like services is "file swapping" or "file sharing," instead of what it truly is-file copying. This is an important distinction, because true "swapping" or "sharing" is protected under current copyright law under a doctrine known as the "first sale" doctrine. Under this doctrine, a person is entitled to "sell or otherwise dispose of" a legally obtained copy of a work, forming the basis for an entire industry of stores selling used books, records, movies, and video games. However, the first sale doctrine only applies to true swapping or sharing; that is, the person who owns the copy must surrender it in order to get a different copy or cash in exchange. The key is that this doctrine applies to a particular copy, but does not give consumers the right to make and pass along additional copies of a work on their own. In the digital environment, that element of swapping or sharing no longer exists.

One implication of the perfect replication and easy Internet distribution of the current era is that a file can spread like a virus. One unprotected copy can lead to two, which leads to four, and so on until the file has spread around the globe. This means that it is no longer good enough to keep a very tight technological lid on copyrighted content. Even if content is protected with the best copy protection technology, "in-the-clear" copies can still find their way to the Internet. These copies sometimes come from within-employees of the record labels or movie studios steal the content from the inside and make it available on the Internet.

Movies can be copied by pointing a digital camcorder at a movie screen. High-quality copies of songs and videos can also be created on playback. For instance, by placing a microphone in a soundproof room and playing a song on an expensive stereo system, a reasonably highquality copy can be made; though this method of copying requires significant expense and effort, "viral spread" means that only one person needs to be willing to do this and the file is forever available. Because potential pirates are everywhere in the production and distribution chain, and because no copyright protection scheme is perfect, the reality of viral spread undercuts even the best copyright protection technologies.

Development of Digital Piracy

Many otherwise law-abiding citizens who would never even consider shoplifting a CD from a store at the mall see nothing wrong with downloading music for free. Indeed, the wide availability of music on the Internet has created a culture where some consumers justify illegal copying as a rebellion against "greedy corporations." One reason for this is that users have come to expect the Internet to provide content for free that would be paid for in the offline environment, such as newspapers and magazines.

Consumer-oriented media products closely tie the content and the media together, allowing consumers to mistakenly assign the value to the media itself. Consumers may believe, therefore, that the DVD itself is the expensive item that is morally off limits for theft, but the movie recorded on that disc is an unlimited resource which is acceptable to take without paying. This, of course, is a gross misconception. The culture of piracy is also fostered by the anonymity of the Internet. Because there is little risk of detection, even those consumers who fully understand that it is wrong to download content without paying for it will do so anyway.

Millions of others are doing it as well, without ever needing to face the consequences, reinforces the attitude that the person doing the stealing is just one of a faceless crowd who will never get caught. In addition, the culture of piracy is encouraged by a significant number of cyber libertarians who espouse an ideology that denies the legitimacy of the concept of copyrights, preferring instead to think information cannot be property. Less extreme are legal scholars, who employ rhetoric about fair use and the limits of copyright law to create a general sense that the widespread file copying taking place on peer-to-peer networks is somehow more legitimate than efforts to stop the piracy from occurring. Added to that are cyber vigilantes who feel that the major labels and studios have colluded to keep prices high in the past, and piracy is a justified response to what they see as corporate malfeasance. Taken together, there is a widespread culture of digital piracy that to date has not been countered with social opprobrium-a clear and unambiguous signal that downloading content for free is wrong.

One frequent misconception about the growth of digital technology for distributing content is that it can simply be matched by equal advances in copyright protection technology. Just as Macrovision served as a fairly effective protection for video cassettes in the analog environment, digital technologies should be able to protect digital content. This is not necessarily the case. Determined pirates have many methods of making illegal copies, and Internet distribution and viral spread take over to make the content widely available. Moreover, hackers and thieves seeking to steal digital content can usually move more quickly than the multi-industry task forces that must come together to create copy protection technologies.

The easiest way for pirated content to be made available on the Internet is to "rip" a CD or DVD. Doing so involves varying degrees of difficulty. For example, DVDs have been protected from the outset by encryption technology that prevents unauthorised access and copying. Because the Digital Millennium Copyright Act (DMCA) makes it illegal to circumvent such access control measures, hacker-created software is necessary to get in-the-clear copies. At the other end of the spectrum are files like older music CDs that contain no copy protection; software to rip the files into downloadable format is widely available from commercial producers.

In other cases, such as programmes broadcast on pay cable channels, the content is protected by "conditional access" technologies to ensure that it cannot be viewed by non-subscribers, but is essentially in the-clear when received by a paying customer and is thus vulnerable to being digitised and posted on the Internet. In all cases, of course, making the files available online in a peer-to-peer network is illegal. Most people who make copies of content do not care if it is legal or not, because the chance of getting caught and punished is so low. The technical hurdles presented by copy protection schemes are rarely a major concern either; hackers routinely crack encryption and distribute files.

Though most content is now sold to consumers in digital format, most of the playback devices-speakers, monitors, television sets-are still analog devices. Therefore the digital-to-analog (D/A) converter is a primary component in every multimedia device. Since most copy protection schemes are digital, and because the digital protections are generally lost when a digital file is converted to analog format for viewing, this creates an "analog hole" in digital copy protection schemes whereby the signal can be captured after conversion to analog and then redigitised in an unprotected form using a readily available analog-to-digital (A/D) converter. This is a relatively simple option for those who don't have the skill or inclination to circumvent standard copy protection. Though doing so involves some degradation in quality, the resulting copy is more than serviceable, and after the initial redigitisation, future generations of copies will experience no further degradation.

Even if a device features copy protection on all the digital and analog outputs, the content must ultimately be displayed in-the-clear so the consumer can see it or hear it. This means that pirates can get a copy of otherwise encrypted material simply by putting a microphone up to a speaker or pointing a video camera at a television screen. Of course, this can involve a serious degradation in quality-an entire episode of Seinfeld focused on the ridiculous effort to create videos of movies in crowded theaters-but under the right circumstances, the resulting copy can be quite good: an empty movie theater or a camcorder that is plugged into the headphone jacks for hearing-impaired patrons, can give perfect audio for a bootleg copy. Though there are some efforts underway to protect against this type of piracy, there is no certainty that the technologies will be effective and, in any case, it will be very difficult to stop this type of piracy in the short run.

Reasons for Copying Digital Content

The issue of illegal file copying might not exist if all copyright owners employed military grade encryption and required consumers to play the content on special devices that made direct copying impossible. There are reasons, however, to encourage the development of advanced copy protection schemes that provide meaningful protection for copyright owners while at the same time allowing flexibility for consumers. For example, there are several legitimate reasons that content might be copied and used without violating copyright law. Locking up content behind airtight technological walls-to the extent that this is even possible-would make those legitimate uses much more difficult, and anger consumers who have come to expect through decades of use that they will be allowed to make copies under certain circumstances. Such measures raise the price of content for law-abiding consumers.

The fair use doctrineis commonly misunderstood and frequently misapplied in the digital copyright debate. Fair use is rather complicated and applies a four-part test to a particular use to determine whether it infringes a copyright. In general, however, fair use is designed to protect specific non-commercial uses of copyrighted material, primarily for educational purposes or purposes of criticism or news reporting. Fair use does not mean, as is commonly supposed, that any copying of copyrighted content is permissible as long as the person doing the copying does not intend to profit from it. At the same time, fair use remains an important part of the balance struck in copyright law.

The fundamental theory underlying copyright is that granting a creator monopoly rights over a creation will encourage innovation and imagination. That monopoly, however, must have certain limitations for creativity to flourish, and fair use is one of these. Protecting content from digital tools that make widespread piracy simple while allowing easy access to content for fair use purposes is a primary challenge of copyright policy in the digital era. It is important, however, to remember that fair use is a balancing factor to copyright, and not an absolute right or a good that must be valued above all others.

Another common reason for copying digital content is to make the use or transmission of that content easier. For example, many large-scale video games sold for home computers can be copied from the CDs on which they are sold to the hard drive of the computer, which makes the games work better. This, however, can also make it easy to install a single copy on multiple machines, generally violating the terms of the license and therefore constituting copyright infringement. Many ISPs also cache copies of frequently requested files on local servers to make Internet traffic run more smoothly for their customers.

Government has recognised the importance of allowing for copies that do nothing more than improve technological efficiency, and has granted an exemption for "ephemeral" copies of works made by broadcasters, webcasters, and distance educators. Content providers themselves also recognise the importance of allowing these uses, and often account for them in their licensing terms. However, fear of piracy may overtake this generally accepting attitude toward copies that enhance efficient operation, and protecting this usage is another key challenge for public policy.

Dating back to the sale of the original phonograph machines, consumers have spent decades building up certain expectations of what they will and will not be allowed to do with the content that they purchase. Technology has changed certain expectations over time; home recording technology, for example, the rise of Napster and its successors have created an unfair expectation of free music available online. In general, however, most consumers have grown comfortable with a set of reasonable uses of content and are angered when their expectations are not met. One example of copyright protection clashing with consumer expectations is the sale of music CDs that can be played in stereo equipment, but not home computers. This prevents illegal ripping of songs, but also confuses consumers who expect that they will be able to play legally purchased CDs as they work at their computers.

Some other widespread consumer expectations for content include device shifting (i.e., being able to purchase and download a song to play on a portable digital music device rather than just on the computer to which the song was downloaded); place shifting (i.e., purchasing a downloaded movie to watch both in the living room and in the back of the minivan); and time shifting (i.e., being able to record a television broadcast to watch at a later time). These expectations have varying degrees of legal protection, but as a practical matter, any successful business model, and indeed copyright law itself, must account for reasonable consumer expectations on the use of the content; failing to do so will only invite piracy.

Technology Options to Protect Copyrights

In order for content providers to continue charging for their products, the legitimate copies must have some advantage over the free copies. That advantage can be created by increasing the hassle of free downloading, the risk of legal penalties for piracy, and the social opprobrium associated with piracy. There are several tools that help meet these goals, and meet them more effectively when accompanied by public policy levers. There are a number of technology options to protect copyrights in the digital environment, with varying support among the many players in business and policy. None are ideal solutions in the sense of being highly effective at a low cost with little degradation in performance. The high number of copyright loopholes and the complexity of the technology make a "silver bullet" solution highly unlikely, if not impossible.

Efforts to develop effective copyright protection technology will work to the extent that the interests of the content producers and the device makers are aligned- both want more content available for sale. However, the incentive to find a solution breaks down if the content providers place too many technical demands on the devices or attempt to limit innovation in media playback devices. By the same token, the incentive to cooperate breaks down if device manufacturers insist upon solutions that are too weak to effectively fight digital piracy. If the right balance is not struck, the incentive for device manufacturers is to stick with the status quo for as long as possible.

Complicating this problem is the presence of self-styled consumer advocacy groups made up of cyber libertarians who want a massive overhaul of copyright law to cut back on intellectual property rights in the digital environment. From a societal perspective, technology solutions should be evaluated with a three-point test: cost to consumers, impact on device performance, and effectiveness. Solutions that are cheap, easy to implement, and highly effective at limiting piracy should always be given priority. In the end, it will be necessary for all parties to compromise on each of these three points if a realistic solution is to be found.

To the greatest extent possible, the compromises should come equally from all three categories; it is not a solution to implement copy controls that only marginally decrease digital piracy, or place an enormous cost on consumers to protect intellectual property owners from theft. Encryption. Broadly speaking, encryption is any technology that scrambles or otherwise makes content unusable unless the consumer possesses the decryption keys necessary to access the content. Use of encryption technologies, from cable descrambler boxes to the Content Scramble System (CSS) on DVDs, is a longstanding strategy for protecting content.

• The primary problem with encryption as a solution to piracy is that it requires the content companies and the technology companies to work together. Unlike many other forms of content protection, encrypted content cannot be sold to consumers unless the playback devices are designed to decrypt it. Because the content creators and the device manufacturers need each other to sell their products, encryption as a strategy takes widespread cooperation across multiple industries.

This need for cooperation was the drive behind the Consumer Broadband and Digital Television Promotion Act, commonly known as the Hollings Bill for its primary sponsor, Sen. Fritz Hollings (D-S.C.). The Hollings Bill would have required the content industries, the hardware/ software industries, and consumer groups to come together to create security system standards and encoding rules for use in the protection of digital content, and then require that all future digital media devices comply with those standards. If the groups did not agree on standards and encoding rules within a year, the federal government would create the standards. This proposal was highly controversial.

The idea of government-designed and mandated security system standards bothered many critics on philosophical grounds, but equally widespread was skepticism that any content protection scheme could be made tamper-proof, as previous efforts had all proven vulnerable to attack. For instance, the CSS system on DVDs entailed full cooperation, because any manufacturer who wished to build DVD players had to incorporate CSS as part of the agreement to license the technology. However, the CSS system was cracked by a teenage hacker, and the code for doing so (called DeCSS) became widely available on the Internet-though most people still refrain from copying DVDs because it is easier to buy a DVD than it is either to use DeCSS to crack a DVD or to download a cracked DVD.

A major industry consortium called the Secure Digital Music Initiative (SDMI) was formed to create copyright protection measures for digital music. The consortium faced much internal disagreement on a variety of subjects, issued a high-profile challenge to hackers to crack their system, and has since quietly faded away. Another problem with encryption technologies is that the encryption disappears once the digital content is converted to an analog signal for playback on media devices. This brings the analog hole problem into play.

An encrypted cable television signal, for instance, is decrypted with a cable box and can then be transferred and copied through the analog output jacks on the consumer's media devices. The easiest way to get around this problem with such "legacy" equipment is to deliver content in a way that won't work on older devices, forcing consumers to either buy new all digital equipment or add new technology to their existing devices. This will be expensive, and would meet with tremendous disapproval from consumers who have recently invested money in high-end media equipment.

Another solution would be to redesign all analog-to-digital conversion devices to take advantage of the new Digital Rights Management (DRM) technologies, a proposition strongly opposed by some companies because they believe it will degrade the performance of the devices. Because the analog hole will remain until most of the existing "legacy" equipment is no longer functional, content providers point out that a solution needs to be devised as quickly as possible to reduce the number of unprotected devices that are on the market. The industries, at the urging of House Commerce Committee Chairman Billy Tauzin (R-La.), are currently at work trying to devise a voluntary solution to the problem.

Encryption remains an effective deterrent against unauthorised copying by the average user does not address the problem of the availability of illegal copies. Several industry consortiums, including the Copy Protection Technical Working Group (CPTWG, pronounced C-P-Twig), the Digital Video Broadcasting Project (DVB), the Moving Pictures Experts Group (MPEG), and many others are actively working on effective content protection technology for a variety of digital media. Such cooperative efforts are a key part of making piracy more difficult. Watermarking and other embedded control technologies. The term watermarking encompasses a variety of technologies, but the basic idea they share is a small piece of code embedded in the digital data stream that will survive the transition from digital to analog and back. Some "forensic" watermarks are designed to reveal the original source of a digital file, making it easier to hunt down and prosecute pirates.

Other watermarks are embedded with the audio or video stream to convey copy protection and usage information to the playback device or the devices used to receive the signal. Another type of embedded control echnology is the "broadcast flag," a signal designed to be embedded in over-the-air broadcasts of digital television and prevent copies of the broadcasts from being distributed on the Internet.

Consumer groups worry that the broadcast flag could eventually be used to prevent not only illegal file duplication, but otherwise permissible network transmissions, like moving a recording from one digital video recorder to another located within the household. The Broadcast Protection Discussion Group of the CPTWG released a report on possible implementation of the broadcast flag, but the conclusions were not unanimous. The Federal Communications Commission is currently considering public comments on the broadcast flag issue, and may advance a regulation that they hope will encourage the content industries to embrace digital television more quickly.

Sen Sam Brownback (R-Kan.) has circulated draft legislation that would (among other things) prohibit the

FCC from requiring a specific technology solution for the broadcast flag, but rather set objective performance standards so that any device that meets the goal of the broadcast flag is compliant. A flexible solution such as this is the best way to implement a broadcast flag because it allows for the flag to be embedded in the signal and requires device manufacturers to read the flag but does not mandate the specific technology that does so.

Forensic watermarks, on the other hand, are a true stand-alone technology; that is, the function of watermarks is not impaired even if there is no cooperation from device manufacturers. But forensic watermarks obviously are not a complete solution. Given enough time, talented hackers can strip some kinds of watermarks from digital signals. Even if the watermarks remain intact, they make it easier to hunt down pirates but do little to prevent the piracy in the first place. Still, watermarking can be an important part of the solution if the implementation is simple, inexpensive, and does not degrade the performance of equipment. Spoofing.

Spoofing is a broad term for selfhelp efforts by content owners that exploit the anonymous nature of file sharing software. When a user logs on to KaZaA or similar programmes, they can search millions of computers for a particular file, then download the file and play it. However, the downloader does not know much about the person from whom the file is being copied.

Spoofing is when the content owners post fake copies of their content, flooding the network with files indistinguishable from pirated copies of the real thing. The flood of spoofs makes finding and downloading a pirated copy much more time consuming, as the downloader is forced to wade through a sea of fakes to find a clean file. Spoofing encompasses a spectrum of progressively more aggressive efforts against downloaders. At its most benign, spoofers simply waste the time of downloaders by forcing them to download multiple files until they find an actual pirated one. With a sufficient flooding of the network, this can encourage downloaders to pay for a legitimate digital download, which they know will be the correct file on the first try.

Unfortunately, file sharing networks tend to be so massive that a flooding spoof attack is unlikely to be effective over the long haul. Further along the spectrum are spoof files that look like music or video files to the untrained eye, but actually contain computer code that can do a number of things-launch a web browser directed to a site where the content can be purchased legally, call back to the content provider to identify the downloader, delete other pirated files on the hard drive, or even freeze up the computer and require the user to restart the machine. Some of these more aggressive spoofing strategies are currently prohibited by antihacking laws, but Rep.

Howard Berman (D-Calif.) introduced legislation last year to allow certain aggressive spoofing strategies. Sen. Orrin Hatch (R-Utah) went even further, suggesting that damaging the computers of pirates "may be the only way you can teach somebody about copyrights." The content industries, however, have shown no interest to date in more aggressive strategies, which led Rep. Berman to abandon his bill. In any case, spoofing definitely increases the hassle of finding pirated content, and in some cases may significantly increase the risk of doing so, which discourages piracy in favour of paying for content. More important, aggressive spoofing impacts only those users who are searching for illegally copied files; it has no impact on law-abiding users.

Law Enforcement

Owners of copyrighted content can turn to both civil courts and the criminal justice system when their property is damaged or stolen. However, the enforcement option has always been timeconsuming and expensive, making it undesirable except for the worst offenders. With the explosion of file copying enabled by the Internet, however, enforcement must become part of the overall strategy to combat piracy. Without effective tools for finding and punishing pirates, copyright holders have only two other options: lock up content using excessively strong methods or refuse to make the content available at all. Either solution ends up punishing law-abiding consumers rather than the individuals who are the cause of the problem.

Though it is illegal to pirate copyrighted material, prosecutions against individuals have been few and far between. Content owners have instead focused their legal efforts on the peer-to-peer networks, without which widespread piracy would be much more difficult. Despite the potential negative public relations involved in suing customers, content providers are starting to do just that. Though there are millions of individuals using peer-to-peer networks for file copying, the content owners can get reasonable results by focusing on those who are making files available for copying.

Most people who pirate files on the internet are willing to download the files, but do not set their software so the files can be uploaded. One study of the Gnutella system showed that 70 percent of the users online did not make their files available for sharing, and that 50 percent of the "hits" to user queries were returned by the top 1 percent of file sharers. The problem is so bad that some current generation networks have tried to attack this problem by rewarding users who make files available for upload with better network performance.

In theory, therefore, attacking that top 1 percent could drastically reduce the piracy on a network, and going after the top 30 percent could effectively destroy the network. Better education about peer-to-peer software can also have an impact on those who do not realise that they are uploading songs to other users because they do not fully understand the default settings of their software. Unfortunately, going after those uploaders is difficult, because peer-to-peer software allows for anonymous connections, and finding the true identity of the uploader is a difficult and costly undertaking.

Going after downloaders is perfectly within the rights of copyright holders as well; in both cases, the increased risk of being punished for copyright infringement makes paying for content more attractive. In September 2003, the Recording Industry Association of America (RIAA) organised a series of lawsuits against some of the most egregious peer-to-peer pirates, many of whom had in excess of 1,000 pirated song files on their computers. Though RIAA suffered an enormous amount of bad publicity for these actions, the procedure is exactly what is necessary to stop individuals from engaging in massive piracy. The individuals targeted by the lawsuits were generally warned in advance that they were being watched, and RIAA has given users the opportunity to delete illegal song files and forswear future piracy in exchange for a pledge from RIAA not to sue. Contrary to much of the public reaction, these lawsuits do not go too far in stopping piracy; they are a measured, reasonable response and are the best option available for increasing the risk and inconvenience of piracy-the suits rightly put the enforcement burden on the property owners and the risk of punishment on the pirates, while sparing law-abiding citizens from intrusive or expensive copyright protection programmes.

The most famous case of legal action against a peer-to-peer network was the lawsuit against Napster, the file sharing software that brought music file copying into the mainstream. Though legal action eventually brought Napster down, the more decentralised nature of the successor peer-to-peer networks makes it harder to stop them through legal action; a recent court ruling held that two distributors of current generation file sharing networks cannot be held legally accountable for the infringement of their users. While that decision is still under appeal, it highlights the difference between Napster and new peer-to-peer networks: Whereas Napster operated centralised servers under the control of the corporation, current file copying programmes such as Morpheus and KaZaA are decentralised, passing queries from user to user rather than through one main server. That means the companies themselves merely distribute the software, but do not participate in the act of copyright infringement the way Napster did.

Though the legal battle is far from settled and many outcomes benefiting rights-holders are possible, it is unlikely that lawsuits will see the same unqualified success against this current generation of software that occurred in the Napster case. Of course, there are also legitimate uses of peer-to-peer networks, most notably for trading media files with the permission of the producer. Garage bands and aspiring filmmakers take advantage of peer-to-peer networks in the hopes of becoming famous, and corporate networks can use such networks to manage their files more efficiently. Because of the substantial noninfringing uses of peer-to-peer networking, it is impossible as a policy matter to simply eliminate the file sharing services, although some amount of regulation might help.

Policy Issues

In the absence of a market failure, it is generally best to let the industry players work together to establish technical standards. This allows the greatest freedom for innovation and balance between competing interests. This principle is especially true in the case of protecting copyrighted digital works, because the challenge is so daunting and the risks are so high. There are no off-the-shelf technologies to resolve the bundle of digital copyright problems; research and development are still needed. It is possible in this case that the interests of all parties will not align sufficiently for a voluntary process to work in a timely manner, or worse, that the technology is simply not capable of preventing large-scale piracy while meeting the three-point test of low cost, low performance degradation, and high effectiveness.

The technological problems can be solved and yet no agreement is forthcoming, it may be necessary for to intervene in the process by altering the incentives of the negotiating parties to arrive at a solution within a mandated time frame. However, it is not yet clear that the voluntary process has been given sufficient time to act, and the short one-year deadline of the Hollings Bill diverted resources to the legislative battle that could have been spent in the standards development process. The government should step back and let current industry groups work toward establishment of solutions, while keeping close track of ongoing progress.

The main downside to a voluntary process is that some manufacturers have an incentive not to comply with the copy protection scheme endorsed by the industry-devices that enable piracy would have a unique selling point. While the federal government should avoid being the body that sets the standards, it is entirely appropriate to mandate compliance with a privately-set standard to eliminate free-riders-those who take advantage of the increased availability of digital content to sell their equipment without accepting responsibility for protecting the content from pirates.

The risk of legal action against online pirates is already very slim due to the sheer volume of illegal downloading occuring on the Internet today. Reducing the risk even further would be counterproductive to the goal of making legal purchases easier than stealing content. Moreover, reducing the tools that content holders have to go after illegal downloaders would increase the pressure for copyright solutions that would impinge on the millions of law-abiding people who do not illegally download music.

Allowing content owners to take steps to disable file copying through the use of spoof files would help to discourage such piracy. Though the language of any such law would have to be carefully worded to prevent damage to machines and Internet infrastructure, the very knowledge that any downloaded file could turn out to be a relatively benign but extremely annoying spoof would make the peer-to-peer networks riskier places to acquire music and video files. Though no content providers are currently pursuing such a strategy, it may become necessary in the future as the piracy problem becomes worse, and a firm legal footing for doing so should be established now.

Because stealing copyrighted material is becoming easier than ever in the networked digital environment, the culture of piracy is taking root in a more damaging way. Journalists carry a certain amount of responsibility for this, by portraying a "balanced" view of the issue that gives the pirates credibility equal to the artists who create the work. Colleges and universities also bear responsibility, as they have largely treated massive piracy on campus networks as a bandwidth issue rather than a criminal activity issue. The attitude that downloading content without paying for it is acceptable must change, and all interested parties-including artists in the entertainment industry-should work together to communicate this message.

The physical distribution of digital content on CDs and DVDs—the manufacture of the disc, printing, packaging, shipping, and retail markup—is a significant expense, accounting for more than half of the cost of a music CD. Selling content over the Internet replaces these costs with less expensive ecommerce costs, but initial business models planned to sell downloadable versions for the same price as the physical copies. That pricing decision cannot be blamed entirely on greed or shortsightedness.

The content industries are facing the same barrier that other industries have faced in making the slow transition to e-commerce: the bricks-and-mortar retailers. The middlemen responsible for selling the physical versions of the product do not want to be undercut by a website selling the same thing for much less, and since the retailers will continue to represent the vast majority of total sales in the early stages of the transition, the content companies must tread carefully to protect their primary distribution outlets. This is a problem already faced by toy manufacturers, book publishers, and other companies that sought to sell their products online and eliminate the middleman. At the extreme, middlemen have used their political influence to strangle online competition, as has happened in the contact lens industry and the automobile industry, or have filed lawsuits, as the National Association of Recording Merchandisers did to Sony to prevent advertising of Sony's e-commerce site in music

CDs. No matter the root causes, the end result is clear: Sales of music have fallen dramatically.

As high-speed Internet connections proliferate, the same fate is likely to befall the video and software industries if they make the same business decisions. Digital distribution can change the economics of content sales, making customers feel they are getting a better value for the amount spent if the savings from eliminating the middlemen is shared with them. A major reason that consumers favour physical distribution over digital distribution is that the old model of purchasing a hard copy at the mall comes with a predictable and flexible set of options: letting a friend borrow the disc for an evening, playing the disc in both the computer and DVD player, making "mix tapes," and so on. Most digital distribution models, in their zeal to prevent illegal file sharing, placed considerable restrictions on what could be done with the files. In the most extreme example, digital music was sold as a subscription service that could only be streamed to a computer that had a live Internet connection.

With such restrictions on use, it is little wonder that consumers turn to the peer-to-peer networks—including those who would gladly pay for the music if they could get it the way they wanted it. This flexibility is so important in the marketplace that there have been numerous calls to mandate it for digital downloads. A group called Digital Consumer has proposed a "Consumer Technology Bill of Rights" that includes a number of flexible uses, such as time shifting digital television broadcasts (recording to watch later) and the right to play legally acquired content on any device.

Rep. Zoe Lofgren (D-Calif.) has introduced the Benefit Authors without Limiting Advancement or Net Consumer Expections (BALANCE) Act to define many of the same rights, including repealing an anti-circumvention provision of the DMCA that will allow consumers to circumvent copyright protection schemes if the use of the content after circumvention is otherwise legal, such as playing a DVD on a computer using a non-Windows operating system.

Sen. Ron Wyden (D-Ore.) has taken a less aggressive approach in the Digital Consumer Right to Know Act, which requires content providers to disclose the limitations imposed by copyright protection measures to consumers before purchase. Though these approaches differ, and while there is disagreement on whether they would achieve their stated aims, the unifying principle is a desire for consumers to have their expectations met with regard to their ability to use digital content while protecting copyright holders from rampant digital piracy.

Of course, some restrictions on the use of digital files will be necessary to ensure that the content providers aren't simply offering a "honey pot" of high-quality digital files that are then freely traded on peer-to-peer networks; new technologies call for new protections. However, retaining flexibility of use as close as possible to what consumers have done with content all their lives will be key to the success of digital distribution.

One of the chief advantages to the retail system of content distribution is that most consumers remain blissfully unaware of which labels or studios produce the music and movies they buy. Consumers can simply walk into a store and look for the name of their favourite band or favourite movie and expect it to be on the shelves, no matter which company produced it. A system where all creative content was sorted by the company that produced it would be extremely ineffective, absent a revolution in the way content is marketed by the producers. Because of this, Internet distribution will not be as effective if each company is left to distribute its products at its own websites. At a minimum, there needs to be a single portal to search for content by title, artist, and so on, even if that site then redirects the consumer to a company's online store. Ideally, however, all of the companies would be allowed to put their wares in a single place where consumers could buy them. Though industry-supported portal sites are the wave of the future for e-commerce, many companies are reluctant to become involved because of the threat of antitrust action by the federal government. The experience of Orbitz, the portal site for the airline industry, is instructive.

The airlines developed a single place for consumers to search for airfares, with the condition that all participating airlines had to make their lowest fares available to the portal, a move made advantageous by the elimination of payments to middlemen in the ticketing and travel agent industries. As a result of pressure from both online and offline competitors, intense antitrust scrutiny followed, and while Orbitz continued operating until ultimately being cleared by the U.S. Department of Justice, it has been a cautionary tale for other industries. Indeed, the Movies.com joint venture between just two studios-Fox Entertainment Group and the Walt Disney Company-fell apart due to antitrust scrutiny by the Department of Justice.

Policymakers need to recognise that, from an antitrust perspective, collaboration by producers is different than collaboration by distributors. The primary reason is that producers build their profit margins into the wholesale cost and are not looking to gain additional profit by maintaining a high-cost distribution process; rather, the incentives on producers is to find the widest, deepest, and cheapest distribution channels for their content. In contrast, if middlemen collaborate to develop a portal, they have a stake in protecting their existing business models and extracting monopoly rents.

5

Cyber Terrorism

Cyber terrorism is the convergence of cyber space and terrorism. It refers to unlawful attacks and threats of attacks against computers, networks and the information stored therein when done to intimidate or coerce a government or its people in furtherance of political or social objectives. Further, to qualify as cyber terrorism, an attack should result in violence against persons or property, or at least cause enough harm to generate fear. Attacks that lead to death or bodily injury, explosions, or severe economic loss would be examples. Serious attacks against critical infrastructures could be acts of cyber terrorism, depending on their impact. Attacks that disrupt nonessential services or that are mainly a costly nuisance would not.

It is important to distinguish between cyber terrorism and "hacktivism," a term coined by scholars to describe the marriage of hacking with political activism. Hacktivists have four main weapons at their disposal:

1. virtual blockades;
2. e-mail attacks;
3. hacking and computer break-ins; and
4. computer viruses and worms.

A virtual blockade is the virtual version of a physical sit-in or blockade: political activists visit a website and attempt to generate so much traffic toward the site that other users cannot reach it, thereby disrupting normal operations while winning publicity-via media reports-for the protesters' cause.

Swarming occurs when a large number of individuals simultaneously access a website, causing its collapse. Swarming can also amplify the effects of the hacktivists' second weapon: e-mail bombing campaigns. Maura Conway reported in her essay "Reality Bytes" on an e-mail bombing campaign launched in July 1997 against the Institute for Global Communications (IGC), a San Francisco-based Internet Service Provider (ISP) that hosted the web pages of Euskal Herria, a publication edited by supporters of the Basque separatist group ETA. The attackers wanted ETA's site removed from the internet. They bombarded IGC's website with thousands of e-mails, clogging the system, and threatened to attack other organisations using IGC services. IGC pulled the Euskal Herria site just a few days later. The Spanish government was suspected of being behind the e-mail bombing, but the identity of the attackers remains uncertain. Whether or not the suspicion is well founded, it underlines the fact that the hacktivists' tools are widely available and can be as easily employed by governments as by small groups of political activists.

Many cyber protesters use the third weapon in the hacktivists' arsenal: web hacking and computer break-ins. In her report "Is Cyber Terror Next?", Denning notes that the Computer Emergency Response Team Coordination Center (CERT/CC), a US-funded research and development center operated by Carnegie Mellon University, reported 2,134 cases of computer break-ins and hacks in 1997. The number of incidents rose to 21,756 in

2000 and to almost 35,000 during the first three quarters of 2001 alone. In 2003, CERT/CC received more than half a million e-mail messages and more than nine hundred hotline calls reporting incidents or requesting information. In the same year, no fewer than 137,529 computer security incidents were reported. Given that many, perhaps most, incidents are never reported to CERT/CC or any agency or organisation, the actual figures are probably much higher. Moreover, Denning notes that each single incident that is reported involves thousands of victims. This rise in cyber attacks reflects the growing popularity of the internet, the vast number of vulnerable targets, and the development of sophisticated and easy-to-use hacking tools.

The fourth category of hacktivist weaponry comprises viruses and worms, both of which are forms of malicious code that can infect computers and propagate over computer networks. Their impact can be enormous. The Code Red worm, for example, infected about a million servers in July 2001 and caused $2. 6 billion in damage to computer hardware, software, and networks, and the I LOVE YOU virus unleashed in 2000 affected more than twenty million internet users and caused billions of dollars in damage. Although neither the Code Red worm nor the I LOVE YOU virus was spread with any political goals in mind (both seem to have been the work of hackers, not hacktivists), some computer viruses and worms have been used to propagate political messages and, in some cases, cause serious damage.

Hacktivism, although politically motivated, does not amount to cyber terrorism. Hacktivists do want to protest and disrupt; they do not want to kill or maim or terrify. However, hacktivism does highlight the threat of cyber terrorism, the potential that individuals with no moral restraint may use methods similar to those developed by hackers to wreak havoc. Moreover, the line between cyber terrorism and hacktivism may sometimes blur, especially if terrorist groups are able to recruit or hire computer-savvy hacktivists or if hacktivists decide to escalate their actions by attacking the systems that operate critical elements of the national infrastructure, such as electric power networks and emergency services.

Development of Cyber Terrorism

The roots of the notion of cyber terrorism can be traced back to the early 1990s, when the rapid growth in internet use and the debate on the emerging "information society" sparked several studies on the potential risks faced by the highly networked, high-tech dependent United States. As early as 1990, the US National Academy of Sciences began a report on computer security with the words,

> "We are at risk. Increasingly, America depends on computers. . . . Tomorrow's terrorist may be able to do more damage with a keyboard than with a bomb. " At the same time, the prototypical term "electronic Pearl Harbor" was coined, linking the threat of a computer attack to an American historical trauma. Psychological, political, and economic forces have combined to promote the fear of cyber terrorism. From a psychological perspective, two of the greatest fears of modern time are combined in the term "cyber terrorism. "

Although cyber terrorism does not entail a direct threat of violence, its psychological impact on anxious societies can be as powerful as the effect of terrorist bombs. Moreover, the most destructive forces working against an understanding of the actual threat of cyber terrorism are a fear of the unknown and a lack of information or, worse, too much misinformation. After 9/11, the security and terrorism discourse soon featured cyber terrorism prominently. This was understandable, given that more nightmarish attacks were expected and that cyber terrorism seemed to offer Al Qaeda opportunities to inflict enormous damage. But there was also a political dimension to the new focus on cyber terrorism. Debates about national security, including the security of cyber space, always attract political actors with agendas that extend beyond the specific issue at hand and the debate over cyber terrorism was no exception to this pattern.

Combating cyber terrorism has become not only a highly politicised issue but also an economically rewarding one. An entire industry has emerged to grapple with the threat of cyber terrorism: think tanks have launched elaborate projects and issued alarming white papers on the subject, experts have testified tc cyber terrorism's dangers before Congress, and private companies have hastily deployed security consultants and software designed to protect public and private targets. Following the 9/11 attacks, the federal government requested $4. 5 billion for infrastructure security, and the FBI now boasts more than one thousand "cyber investigators. "

The evolution of cyber terrorism can be analysed by examining how access to cyber technology is perceived and used by terrorist groups. Two views of the subject are presented by Schmitt and Rathmell. Schmitt distinguishes between information operations and computer network attacks. The former is defined as encompassing "virtually any nonconsensual actions intended to discover, alter, destroy, disrupt, or transfer data stored in a computer, manipulated by a computer, or transmitted through a computer network. " Information systems can be either defensive or offensive in nature. Computer network attacks are considered offensive information operations and "disrupt, deny, degrade, or destroy information resident in computers and computer networks, or the computers and networks themselves. "

Rathmell identifies three categories of information warfare that can be used by sub-state groups. These are:

- *Category I* - new techniques applied to traditional activities in the form of intelligence gathering, communication, money laundering and propaganda. All substate groups have to engage in these to survive;
- *Category II* - old techniques applied to new activities. This involves using physical violence against the information activities of a target entity. Increasing reliance of all of these entities [armies, governments, nation-states or companies] on information activities enables a sub-state group to leverage its limited resources into a damaging attack; and
- *Category III* - new techniques applied to new activities. This involves using digital attack techniques against the information activities of a target entity and is perhaps the purest form of IW. Let us consider two primary components of cyber terrorism, terrorist employment of computers for non-violent activity that facilitates, but falls short of terrorism, and terrorist activity where computer technology is a specific component (weapon or target) of a terrorist incident.

IT as a Tool of Terrorists

Terrorist groups increasingly use computer technology to secure many of their organisational goals. In this sense, terrorist groups are simply exploiting modern tools to accomplish the same goals they sought in the past. The difference between conventional terrorist tactics and those involving computers can be found in three key ingredients: ease of operations; developing potential; and increased anonymity. None of these activities are easily detected or readily countered and thus, enable terrorist groups that take advantage of computer technology to create viable support structures to further their tactical and strategic goals. These are accomplished through:

- political propaganda
- recruitment
- financing
- intra and inter-group communication and coordination
- information/intelligence gathering
- stealth/anonymity in both routine activity and tactical operations
- ease of operations that are "cost effective" both in terms of resources expended and ability to strike world-wide.

Examples of the facilitation of terrorism through the use of computer technology illustrate the appeal this technology has for terrorist groups interested in advancing their particular agendas. The use of the internet for propaganda and disinformation purposes is an especially popular one.

Many exiled political opposition groups emanating from such states as Iran, Iraq, Mexico, Northern Ireland and Saudi Arabia have used the World Wide Web for just such purposes. Neo-Nazi groups, the Colombian ELN, Hezbollah and Zapatistas have also adopted similar tactics. One of the most demonstrative examples, however, involves the case of the December, 1996 takeover of the Japanese Ambassador's residence in Lima, Peru by the Tupac Amaru Revolutionary Movement (MRTA). Not only did this terrorist group use the internet to communicate its revolutionary message to the rest of the world through a European website, it even offered a video clip of its members preparing for their mission. The added attractiveness of the internet for terrorists is that the widest possible audience for their violent activity not only reiterates the major themes of their campaigns, it also heightens fear in the target audience by reminding it of the potential for future violence.

The nature of modern computer technology is such that it also lends itself to the communication and intelligence activities of terrorist groups. The attractiveness of this feature for groups eager to expand their activities can be explained as follows:

> IT [Information Technology] gives individuals and groups a reach and influence that was previously reserved for well-organised, state-funded terrorist organisations. It represents, in many respects, the 'death of distance'. Physical distance and national borders that once separated terrorists from their co-conspirators, their audience and their targets cease to exist in the world of modern telecommunications and the internet.

Modern computer technology has not only enhanced much of the terrorist activity, but has done so in such a fashion that the terrorist groups that utilise it are now able to operate beyond the purview of traditional counter terrorist approaches. The terrorist ability to engage in "growth activity", such as recruitment, communication and especially financing without the knowledge of state authorities may inevitably lead to stronger and hence, more resilient terrorist groups. In turn, the potential for terrorist groups to engage in activity that focuses less on threats and more on tangible actions is significantly heightened.

Modern terrorist groups that are able to develop undetected may become stronger, more elusive and deadlier than their earlier counterparts. Moreover, and perhaps even more importantly the advent of computer networks has spawned a new direction in the organisational structure of terrorist groups. Terrorist groups utilising computers for communication are likely to move beyond hierarchical organisational structures and employ networked ones.

Terrorist groups engaging in cyber terrorism are noted for threats to commerce, public safety and national security. These threats can take any number of forms, but are generally parlayed into computer versus computer confrontations Terrorist groups use their own computer technology to threaten or attack a victim's computer resources. This can take the form of threats or attacks against national infrastructures that have become heavily reliant and interconnected to computer networks. Activity of this sort is tangible in nature and thus, generates most of the interest we have in cyber terrorism today. Cyber terrorist threats can include:

- rapid communication of threats to a wide or specific audience
- threats to public utilities and transportation
- threats to commercial institutions and transnational corporations
- threats to IGOs and NGOs
- threats to individuals
- threats to political groups or other ethnic, religious or nationalist entities identified as "the enemy"
- threats to security forces
- threats to nation states

What we occasionally see is actual damage to the above targets in the form of temporary disruption of services,public inconveniences or financial loss. These incidents, however, are most often in the form of cyber crime and fall short of what is considered as cyber terrorism.

Cyber Terrorism Threats

Many studies have dealt with terrorism by examining the nature of terrorist group characteristics and their resultant behavior. Few, however, have taken into account how the cyber environment will impact this behavior. In order to assess accurately the nature of the terrorist threat in this decade, it is imperative to include the significance of this factor into future analyses. Part of the "mystique" of terrorism can be understood by identifying the profile of actions or motivations that drive the actions of various terrorist groups. Each group has a relatively unique identity that helps to define how it will behave. While it is unlikely that the emergence of computer technology will radically reshape the essence of why certain terrorist groups choose to exist, the convergence of this technology along with a number key political and social changes will ultimately be reflected in a "new terrorist agenda. "

Perhaps the most profound environmental change to affect the course of terrorism in the last decade has been the collapse of the former Soviet Union. The end of the cold war and the rise of the present American hegemony has had important implications for the many political ideologies that have encouraged and sustained terrorist campaigns over the last forty years. In particular, the goal of a left-backed global revolution is no longer tenable. At the same time, the demise of all but a few communist states has eliminated the raison d'être of many right-wing groups whose existence depended upon their identification as the bulwark of anti-communism

The ideological void faced by terrorist groups of the twenty-first century has not, however, led to the demise of terrorism. In contrast to earlier periods where leftist or Marxist ideologies were mistakenly characterised as the greatest source of international terrorism, religious identity has now taken center stage. Nationalist and ethnic sources which were always a prominent, but less emphasised aspect of terrorist motivations continue in importance. Nationalist and ethnic ambitions have been further accentuated by regional conflicts, some of which have also developed along religious lines. Despite noteworthy changes in the global political environment, non-state terrorism continues.

The ability of terrorist groups to capitalise on modern computer technology is now a requisite for developing the underlying basis for effective and robust activity. In previous decades, terrorist groups were initially constrained because the accumulation of sizeable resources was inevitably linked to sufficient manpower and the ability to keep growth activities clandestine. The recent introduction of computer technology has not lessened the need to accumulate similar resources, but has had major implications for how they are accrued. In order to succeedin what can only be described as an increasingly competitive political and social environment, terrorists groups must ensure that they are able to develop the appropriate infrastructure to continue to operate on a regular basis. Groups that fail to do so will not survive.

The opportunities presented by the cyber environment to what would otherwise be marginally viable terrorist groups has translated into more groups that are less reliant on external sponsors. As a terrorist group's freedom from sponsorship grows, so does its freedom to pursue a truly idiosyncratic campaign of terrorism. The question of terrorist behavior as it relates to the cyber environment has yet to be answered with any certitude as little research emphasis has been placed on explaining how various types of terrorist groups will approach and exploit evolving computer technology. In order to proceed with the analysis of cyber terrorism and terrorist group behavior a small, but functional typology has been created with the intent of identifying basic terrorist group characteristics which are thought to influence much of their activity. The typology is composed of four classes of terrorist group which are currently active and are likely to develop their own sets of cyber modus operandi. The four classes of terrorist group comprising the typology and relevant examples of these groups are as follows:

1. *Nationalist/Ethnic* (Basque Fatherland and Liberty - Military Wing (ETA-M), Provisional Wing of the Irish Republican Army (PIRA), Liberation Tigers of Tamil Eelam (LTTE));
2. *Religious* (Armed Islamic Group (GIA), Aum Supreme Truth - Aum Shinrikyo (Aum), Egyptian Islamic Jihad);
3. *Political* (Covenant, the Sword and the Arm of the Lord (CSA), Revolutionary Organisation 17 November (17 November), Tupac Amaru Revolutionary Movement (MRTA));
4. *Single Issue* (Animal Liberation Front (ALF), Earth Liberation Front, People for the Ethical Treatment of Animals (PETA)).

Each class of group varies from one another in terms of motivation, size, age, parliamentary representation, political constituency, enemy and theatre of operations. In a conventional environment the features of a terrorist group will either retard or enhance what a group is willing and capable of conducting. In a cyber environment the same rationale applies with the caveat that access to computers and computer networks add a new dimension to how group behavior is determined.

The extent of change in terrorist group behavior from conventional to cyber settings is dependent on the degree to which the groups desire and are able to interface with their new tool of choice. At least two initial observations can be made in this regard.

First, terrorist groups will universally adopt those aspects of the cyber environment that will enable them to operate and grow with a greater degree of efficiency. This is to say that all types of terrorist groups stand to benefit from improved communication skills whether they are used purely for propaganda purposes, act as new vehicles of financial growth, or are even used more discreetly for intra/inter group conferencing.

The second observation centres on how each class of terrorist group will move beyond the relatively "simple" task of using computers for non-violent purposes to actually engage in cyber terrorism. The degree to which terrorist groups embrace computer technology as weapon of choice remains to be seen. At one level, the use of cyber technology for inflicting harm on a victim requires a greater level of sophistication than merely using the same technology for communication or propaganda. Not only, must there be some level of expertise in translating the "raw" cyber technology into a weapon of destruction, there must be a recognition that the effectiveness of this alternative supercedes conventional options. Simply stated, a cyber attack against an opponent should produce similar or greater results for less effort than a conventional one.

With the growing interconnectedness of infrastructures relying on cyber technology, the targeting selection of cyber terrorism is likely to be significantly influenced by those targets that allow for a maximum level of disruption. The same, however, is not necessarily true with respect to the mode of attack. Cyber technology allows for an addition variable to be introduced into tactical equations, but clearly represents a single choice in terms of overall modes of operation.

While the study of terrorism routinely exaggerates such acts as assassinations, bombings, hijackings and kidnappings, these events account for a relatively small portion of what occurs within the rubric of the terrorism experience and are meaningless if they are not understood in terms of their overall consequences. The same is true with respect to cyber terrorism. The rapidly emerging cyber environment brings many concerns and uncertainties. Modern computer technology is such that it offers contemporary terrorist groups a wide range of opportunities to continue their campaigns of violence and if they are proficient, significantly further their political objectives.

For the most part, computer technology will play a major role in providing a wider range of options for terrorist growth potential. While this is not cyber terrorism per se, it does have critical implications for the future of both conventional and cyber terrorism. The fact that group infrastructures will evolve to mirror these changes is also a salient concern. Developments in the organisational structure of terrorist groups will not only test existing counter terrorist intelligence efforts, but will undoubtedly facilitate new and potentially unconventional terrorist group alliances.

Rise of Networked errorist Groups

The information age is affecting not only the types of targets and weapons terrorists choose, but also the ways in which such groups operate and structure their organisations. Several of the most dangerous terrorist organisations are using information technology (IT)—such as computers, software, telecommunication devices, and the internet —to better organise and coordinate dispersed activities. Like the large numbers of private corporations that have embraced IT to operate more efficiently and with greater flexibility, terrorists are harnessing the power of IT to enable new operational doctrines and forms of organisation. And just as companies in the private sector are forming alliance networks to provide complex services to customers, so too are terrorist groups "disaggregating" from hierarchical bureaucracies and moving to flatter, more decentralised, and often changing webs of groups united by a common goal.

The rise of networked terrorist groups is part of a broader shift to what Arquilla and Ronfeldt have called "netwar." Netwar refers to an emerging mode of conflict and crime at societal levels, involving measures short of traditional war in which the protagonists are likely to consist of dispersed, small groups who communicate, coordinate, and conduct their campaigns in an internetted manner, without a precise central command. Netwar differs from modes of conflict in which the actors prefer formal, stand-alone, hierarchical organisations, doctrines, and strategies, as in past efforts, for example, to build centralised revolutionary movements along Marxist lines.

Today, in the business world, virtual or networked organisations are heralded as effective alternatives to traditional bureaucracies because of their inherent flexibility, adaptiveness, and ability to capitalise on the talents of all of their members. Networked organisations share three basic sets of features. First, communication and coordination are not formally specified by horizontal and vertical reporting relationships, but rather emerge and change according to the task at hand. Similarly, relationships are often informal and marked by varying degrees of intensity, depending on the needs of the organisation. Second, internal networks are usually complemented by linkages to individuals outside the organisation, often spanning national boundaries. Like internal connections, external relationships are formed and wind down according to the life cycle of particular joint projects. Third, both internal and external ties are enabled not by bureaucratic fiat, but rather by shared norms and values, as well as by reciprocal trust. Internally, the bulk of the work is conducted by self-managing teams, while external linkages compose "a constellation involving a complex network of contributing firms or groups".

What has been emerging in the business world is now becoming apparent in the organisational structures of the newer and more active terrorist groups, which appear to be adopting decentralised, flexible network structures. The rise of networked arrangements in terrorist organisations is part of a wider move away from formally organised, state-sponsored groups to privately financed, loose networks of individuals and subgroups that may have strategic guidance but that, nonetheless, enjoy tactical independence. For example, in the Greater Middle East, terrorist organisations have diverse origins, ideologies, and organisational structures but can be categorised roughly into traditional and new-generation groups. Traditional groups date to the late 1960s and early 1970s, and the majority were formally or informally linked to the Palestine Liberation Organisation (PLO). Typically, they are also relatively bureaucratic and maintain a nationalist or Marxist agenda. These groups have utilised autonomous cells as part of their organisational structure, but the operation of such cells is guided by a hierarchy through clear reporting relationships and virtually little horizontal coordination.

In contrast, the newer and less hierarchical groups (such as Hamas; the Palestinian Islamic Jihad; Hizbollah; Algeria's Armed Islamic Group; the Egyptian Islamic Group; and Osama bin Laden's terrorist network, al-Qaeda) have become the most active organisations. In these loosely organised groups with religious or ideological motives, operatives are part of a network that relies less on bureaucratic fiat and more on shared values and horizontal coordination mechanisms to accomplish its goals. The new and more active generation of Middle Eastern groups has operated both inside and outside the region. For instance, in Israel and the occupied territories, Hamas and to a lesser extent the Palestinian Islamic Jihad have demonstrated their strength over the last five years with a series of suicide bombings that have killed more than 100 people. In Egypt, the Islamic Group carried out a 1997 attack at Luxor, killing 58 tourists and four Egyptians. Another string of terrorist attacks has focused attention on a loosely organised group of "Arab Afghans"-radical Islamic fighters from several North African and Middle Eastern countries who have forged ties while resisting the Soviet occupation of Afghanistan. One of the leaders and founders of the Arab Afghan movement is Osama bin Laden, a Saudi entrepreneur based in Afghanistan.

To varying degrees, these groups share the principles of the networked organisation-relative flatness, decentralisation and delegation of decisionmaking authority, and loose lateral ties among dispersed groups and individuals. Hamas, for example, is loosely structured with some elements working clandestinely and others working openly through mosques and social service institutions to recruit members, raise money, organise activities, and distribute propaganda. The pro-Iranian Hizbollah in southern Lebanon acts as an umbrella organisation of radical Shiite groups and in many respects is a hybrid of hierarchical and network arrangements—although the organisational structure is formal, interactions among members are volatile and do not follow rigid lines of control. Perhaps the most interesting example of a terrorist netwar actor is Osama bin Laden's complex network of relatively autonomous groups that are financed from private sources. Bin Laden uses his wealth and organisational skills to support and direct al-Qaeda (The Base), a multinational alliance of Islamic extremists.

Al-Qaeda seeks to counter any perceived threats to Islam—wherever they come from—as indicated by bin Laden's 1996 declaration of a holy war against the United States and the West in general. In the declaration, bin Laden specified that such a holy war was to be waged by irregular, light, highly mobile forces. Although bin Laden finances al-Qaeda and directs some operations, he apparently does not play a direct command-and-control role over all operatives. Rather, he is a key figure in the coordination and support of several dispersed nodes. There are reports that communications between al-Qaeda's members combine elements of a "hub-and-spoke" structure and a wheel structure. Al-Qaeda's command-and-control structure includes a consultation council, which discusses and approves major undertakings, and possibly a military committee.

At the heart of al-Qaeda is bin Laden's inner core group, which sometimes conducts missions on its own. Most of the other member organisations remain independent, although the barriers between them are permeable. According to U. S. District Court testimony in New York, al-Qaeda has forged alliances with Egypt's Islamic Group, the National Front in the Sudan, the government of Iran, and Hizbollah. Media reports also indicate that bin Laden has ties with other far-flung Islamic armed groups, such as Abu Sayyaf in the Philippines, as well as with counterparts in Somalia, Chechnya, and Central Asia. Lateral coordination mechanisms facilitate the operations of networked groups. In turn, such coordination mechanisms are enabled by advances in information technology—including increases in the speed of communication, reductions in the costs of communication, increases in bandwidth, vastly expanded connectivity, and the integration of communication and computing technologies. More specifically, new communication and computing technologies allow the establishment of networks in three critical ways. First, new technologies have greatly reduced transmission time, enabling dispersed organisational actors to communicate and coordinate their tasks. This phenomenon is not new in the early 20th century, the introduction of the telephone made it possible for large corporations to decentralise their operations through local branches. Second, new technologies have significantly reduced the cost of communication, allowing information-intensive organisational designs such as networks to become viable.

In the past, organisations sought to reduce coordination and communications costs by centralising and colocating those activities that are inherently more coordination-intensive. With the lowering of coordination costs, it is becoming increasingly possible to further disaggregate organisations through decentralisation and autonomy. Third, new technologies have substantially increased the scope and complexity of the information that can be shared, through the integration of computing with communications. Such innovations as tele and computer conferencing, groupware, internet chat, and web sites allow participants to have "horizontal" and rich exchanges without requiring them to be located in close proximity. Thus, information-age technologies are highly advantageous for a netwar group whose constituents are geographically dispersed or carry out distinct but complementary activities.

Using the internet for communication can increase speed of mobilisation and allow more dialogue between members, which enhances the organisation's flexibility, since tactics can be adjusted more frequently. Individuals with a common agenda and goals can form subgroups, meet at a target location, conduct terrorist operations, and then readily terminate their relationships and redisperse. The bin Laden network appears to have adopted information technology to support its networked mode of operations. According to reporters who visited bin Laden's headquarters in a remote mountainous area of Afghanistan, the terrorist financier has modern computer and communications equipment. Bin Laden allegedly uses satellite phone terminals to coordinate the activities of the group's dispersed operatives and has even devised countermeasures to ensure his safety while using such communication systems.

Satellite phones reportedly travel in separate convoys from bin Laden's; the Saudi financier also refrains from direct use, often dictating his message to an assistant, who then relays it telephonically from a different location. Bin Laden's operatives have used CD-ROM disks to store and disseminate information on recruiting, bomb making, heavy weapons, and terrorist operations. Egyptian computer experts who fought alongside bin Laden in the Afghan conflict are said to have helped him devise a communications network that relies on the web, email, and electronic bulletin boards so that members can exchange information. This is a trend found among other terrorist actors in the Middle East.

Counterterrorist operations targeting Algerian Armed Islamic Group (GIA) bases in the 1990s uncovered computers and diskettes with instructions for the construction of bombs. In fact, it has been reported that the GIA makes heavy use of floppy disks and computers to store and process orders and other information for its members, who are dispersed in Algeria and Europe. The militant Islamic group Hamas also uses the internet to share and communicate operational information. Hamas activists in the United States use chat rooms to plan operations and activities. Operatives use email to coordinate actions across Gaza, the West Bank, and Lebanon. Hamas has realised that information can be passed relatively securely over the internet because counterterrorism intelligence cannot accurately monitor the flow and content of all internet traffic. In fact, Israeli security officials cannot easily trace Hamas messages or decode their content.

Terrorist networks can protect their vital communication flows through readily available commercial technology, such as encryption programs. Examples from outside the Middle East point in this direction-according to one report, Animal Liberation Front (ALF) cells in North America and Europe use the encryption program Pretty Good Privacy (PGP) to send coded email and share intelligence. New encryption programs emerging on the commercial market are becoming so sophisticated that coded emails may soon be extremely difficult to break. In fact, strong encryption programs are being integrated into commercial applications and network protocols so that soon encryption will be easy and automatic.

Rumours persist that the French police have been unable to decrypt the hard disk on a portable computer belonging to a captured member of the Spanish/Basque organisation ETA (Fatherland and Liberty). It has also been suggested that Israeli security forces were unsuccessful in their attempts at cracking the codes used by Hamas to send instructions for terrorist attacks over the internet. Terrorists can also use steganography—a method of hiding secret data in other data such as embedding a secret message within a picture file. Terrorists can also encrypt cell phone transmissions, steal cell phone numbers and program them into a single phone, or use prepaid cell phone cards purchased anonymously to keep their communications secure.

The latest communications technologies are thus enabling terrorists to operate from almost any country in the world, provided they have access to the necessary IT infrastructure; and this affects the ways in which groups rely on different forms of sponsorship. Some analysts have argued that networked terrorists may have a reduced need for state support indeed, governmental protection may become less necessary if technologies such as encryption allow a terrorist group to operate with a greater degree of stealth and safety. Others point to the possibility that groups will increasingly attempt to raise money on the web, as in the case of Pakistan's Lashkar-e-Taiba. To be sure, there are limits to how much reliance terrorist networks will place on information age technology. For the foreseeable future, electronically mediated coordination will not be able to entirely supplant face-to-face exchanges, because uncertainty and risk will continue to characterise most organisational choices and interactions among individuals.

Moreover, informal linkages and the shared values mentioned above—which are critical enablers of networked designs—can only be fostered through personal contact. Electronically mediated exchange can increase the range, amount, and velocity of information flow in a network organisation. But the viability and effectiveness of this electronic network will depend critically on an underlying network of social relationships based on face-to-face interaction. Moreover, while IT-enabled communication flows can greatly help a network coordinate dispersed activities, they can also present a security risk. Communication over electronic channels can become a liability, since it leaves digital "traces." For instance, FBI officials have recently acknowledged that they used an internet wiretap program called "Carnivore" to track terrorist email correspondence at least 25 times.

Acquisition of Offensive Information Capability

IT can improve terrorist intelligence collection and analysis, as well as offensive information operations (IO). The acquisition by terrorist groups of an offensive IO capability could represent a significant threat as the world becomes more dependent on information and communications flows. We argue that information age technology can help terrorists conduct three broad types of offensive IO. First, it can aid them in their perception management and propaganda activities. Next, such technology can be used to attack virtual targets for disruptive purposes. Finally, IT can be used to cause physical destruction. Given the importance of knowledge and soft power to the conduct of netwar, it is not surprising that networked terrorists have already begun to leverage IT for perception management and propaganda to influence public opinion, recruit new members, and generate funding.

Getting a message out and receiving extensive news media exposure are important components of terrorist strategy, which ultimately seeks to undermine the will of an opponent. In addition to such traditional media as television or print, the internet now offers terrorist groups an alternative way to reach out to the public, often with much more direct control over their message. The news media play an integral part in a terrorist act because they are the conduit for news of the violence to the general population.

Terrorism may be seen as a violent act that is conceived specifically to attract attention and then, through the publicity it generates, to communicate a message. Terrorists have improved their media management techniques to the point of using "spin doctoring" tactics. In fact, some groups have even acquired their own television and radio stations to take direct control of the reporting of events. Hizbollah, through its television station, has broadcast footage of strikes carried out by its operatives and has a sophisticated media center that regularly—and professionally—briefs foreign journalists. Hizbollah field units have even included specially designated cameramen to record dramatic video footage of Israeli casualties that was then aired in Lebanon and usually rebroadcast by Israeli television.

The internet now expands the opportunities for publicity and exposure beyond the traditional limits of television and print media. Before the internet, a bombing might be accompanied by a phone call or fax to the press by a terrorist claiming responsibility. Now, bombings can be followed—should terrorists so desire—by an immediate press release from their own web sites. The fact that many terrorists now have direct control over the content of their message offers further opportunities for perception management, as well as for image manipulation, special effects, and deception.

An internet presence could prove advantageous for mobilising "parttime cyber terrorists"—individuals not directly affiliated with a given terrorist group who nonetheless support its agenda and who use malicious software tools and instructions available at a terrorist web site. This scenario would closely resemble the initiatives taken by both the Israeli and Palestinian governments, which have encouraged private citizens to download computer attack tools and become involved in the conflict surrounding the al-Aqsa Intifadah. It appears that nearly all terrorist groups have a web presence. A Hizbollah even manages multiple sites—each with a different purpose. Web sites can also be used to refine or customise recruiting techniques.

Recording which types of propaganda receive the most browser hits could help tailor a message for a particular audience. Using some of the same marketing techniques employed by commercial enterprises, terrorist servers could capture information about the users who browse their web sites, and then later contact those who seem most interested. Recruiters may also use more interactive internet technology to roam online chat rooms and cyber cafes looking for receptive members of the public, particularly young people. Electronic bulletin boards and user nets can also serve as vehicles for reaching out to potential recruits. Interested computer users around the world can be engaged in long-term "cyber relationships" that could lead to friendship and eventual membership.

Netwar-oriented terrorists can also use IT to launch disruptive attacks—that is, electronic strikes that temporarily disable, but do not destroy, physical and/or virtual infrastructure. If the ultimate goal of a terrorist is to influence his opponent's will to fight, IO offer additional means to exert influence beyond using simple physical attacks to cause terror. Disruptive attacks include "choking" computer systems through such tools as e-bombs, fax spamming, and hacking techniques to deface web sites. These strikes are usually nonlethal in nature, although they can wreak havoc and cause significant economic damage.

Disruptive strikes by terrorists have been relatively few and fairly unsophisticated—but they do seem to be increasing in frequency. For example, in 1996, the Liberation Tigers of Tamil Eelam (LTTE) launched an email bomb attack against Sri Lankan diplomatic missions. Using automated tools, the guerilla organisation flooded Sri Lankan embassies with thousands of messages, thus establishing a "virtual blockade. "Japanese groups have allegedly attacked the computerised control systems for commuter trains, paralysing major cities for hours. In 2000, a group of Pakistani hackers who call themselves the Muslim Online Syndicate (MOS) defaced more than 500 web sites in India to protest the conflict in Kashmir . Finally, Pakistan's Lashkare-Taiba claimed to have attacked Indian military web sites in early 2000.

IT-driven information operations can lead to the actual destruction of physical or virtual systems. Malicious viruses and worms can be used to permanently destroy (erase) or corrupt (spoof) data and cause economic damage. In the worst case, these same software tools can be used to cause destructive failure in a critical infrastructure like air traffic control, power, or water systems, which can lead to casualties. Indeed, it is likely that information operations that result in the loss of life may offer the same level of drama as physical attacks with bombs. Also, striking targets through electronic means does not carry the risks associated with using conventional weapons—such as handling explosives or being in close proximity to the target.

The extreme case where the use of IT results in significant human losses has yet to occur. The lack of destructive information attacks is arguably influenced by the relative difficulty of electronically destroying (rather than disrupting) critical infrastructure components—the level of protection of existing infrastructure may be too high for terrorists to overcome with their current IT skill set. In fact, a terrorist organisation would first have to overcome significant technical hurdles to develop an electronic attack capability. Concentrating the necessary technical expertise and equipment to damage or destroy targeted information systems is no easy task, given the computer security risks involved.

In developing and increasing their reliance on electronic attacks, terrorist organisations may be assuming risks and costs associated with the relative novelty of the technology. Terrorists wishing to expand the scope of their offensive IO activities would have to continue upgrading and researching new technologies to keep up with the countermeasures available to computer security experts and systems administrators. This technology "treadmill" would demand constant attention and the diversion of scarce organisational resources.

Another important determinant in netwar terrorists choosing lowlevel IT is that such conventional weapons as bombs remain more cost-effective. In fact, most terrorism experts believe that existing groups see their current tactics as sufficient and are not interested in branching into computer network attacks. Since current tactics are simple and successful, there is no built-in demand to innovate: bombing still works. As long as current tactics enable these groups to accomplish their short-term goals and move toward their longterm goals, there will be no strong incentives to change behavior.

Disruptive attacks may be easier to carry out, but because of their very nature they do not produce the same kind of visceral and emotional reaction that the loss of human life does. Indeed, some terrorism analysts argue that it is unlikely that terrorist groups will turn to disruptive attacks as the primary tactic. Brian Jenkins points out that IT-enabled disruptive strikes do not produce the immediate, visible effects. There is no drama. No lives hang in the balance. Terrorist intentions regarding cyber terrorism are even more problematic. Linking the objectives of actual terrorist groups to scenarios of electronic sabotage that would serve those objectives is conjecture.

Modern Trends in Cyber Terrorism

The available evidence suggests that netwar terrorists have embraced IT for organisational purposes, but they have been either unable or unwilling to attempt more ambitious offensive IO. However, the benefits clearly outweigh the risks when it comes to utilising IT for perception management and propaganda. Were the trends described above to persist, one could speculate that future netwar actors will continue to consolidate their IT use primarily for organisational purposes, with some emphasis on perception management on the offensive IO side. Under these conditions, networked terrorists would still rely on such traditional weapons as conventional bombs to cause physical violence. But they will also transmit information on how to build such weapons via CD-ROMs or email, use chat rooms to coordinate their activities, and use web sites to publicise and justify their strikes to a global audience.

The al-Aqsa Intifadah in the West Bank and Gaza highlights how protracted IO campaigns could be waged in conjunction with a campaign of conventional violence. Mirroring the real-world violence that has resulted in hundreds of casualties, a conflict has also been waged in cyber space over economic and propaganda stakes. Palestinian hackers who support the al-Aqsa Intifadah have been waging a cyber jihad against Israeli government and commercial targets, defacing web sites and conducting DOS attacks. More than 40 Israeli sites have been hit, including the Tel Aviv Stock Exchange and the Bank of Israel. Israeli hackers have counterattacked, hitting more than 15 different Palestinian targets, including Hizbollah, Hamas, and the Palestinian National Authority. As the disruptive attacks have escalated, individuals and groups have joined both sides, from professional hackers to "script-kiddies".

Terrorist access to technologies that can be readily employed without extensive internal development efforts by group members and part-time "volunteers" or through "hackers for hire" will be a critical facilitating factor. Equally important, the relative vulnerability of the information infrastructure plays a role in this calculus. These possible developments would likely prompt the evolution of current netwar terrorist groups toward greater reliance on IT for offensive purposes and could also encourage the emergence of new and completely virtual groups that exclusively operate in cyber space.

The introduction of new technologies in an organisation follows a complex and often lengthy process. Not only do innovative systems have to be developed or acquired, but organisational actors have to become familiar with new systems and be able to use them effectively. Given the challenge, terrorist groups are likely to channel their scarce organisational resources to acquire those IT skills that have the greatest leverage for the least amount of cost and effort. Having access to the internet and cellular telephones is not overly complicated, and it plays a significant role in enabling dispersed operations, a key goal of netwar groups. This reasoning also suggests that over time terrorist groups might begin to experiment more aggressively with information-age technologies for offensive information operations, as they become more familiar with such innovations. The knowledge of IT issues gained by relying on technology to facilitate interactions among group members, or to gain a web presence, might eventually be expanded and harnessed for increasingly offensive uses.

The pace with which current groups move through such a path is also dependent on the degree of cooperation and information exchange among netwar terrorists. Such cooperation has often occurred in the past—for instance,

Islamic radicals have organised "terror conferences", while European terrorist groups such as the Irish Republican Army entered into joint ventures with counterparts across the globe to learn from one another and disseminate knowledge. Given the loose and reciprocal nature of ties between actors in networks such as al-Qaeda, it is entirely possible that those with IT skills would be leveraged globally and placed at the disposal of the organisation's various members.

An alternative hypothesis to the notion that existing terrorist groups should be watched for signs of movement toward cyber terror is that qualitative improvements in the informatisation of networked terrorists will only be witnessed with the emergence of newer, and more technologically savvy, groups. Just as Hamas and al-Qaeda have overshadowed the PFLP and other Marxist groups formed in the 1960s, new-generation groups may further advance the trend toward networked and IT-reliant organisations. New groups could even be led by individuals who are technically skilled, suggesting the rise of a hybrid breed of terrorists cum hackers. Like hackers, they would undertake most of their attacks in cyber space. Like terrorists, they would seek to strike targets by both disruptive and destructive means to further a political or religious agenda.

The possibility that innovation will take place only with the advent of new groups finds support in previous work by such terrorism experts as Hoffman, who describes most groups today as operationally conservative. Aside from organisational inertia, current groups may also be hesitant to further rely on IT for offensive purpose because of large, "sunk costs" in traditional tactics, training, and weapon stockpiles. Existing groups wishing to "amortise" such capital cost may be unwilling to direct scarce resources toward the development of new and radically different offensive techniques.

The acquisition and use of information age technology by terrorist groups are far from certain. Indeed, the scenarios painted above are not mutually exclusive. It is conceivable that current groups will acquire new IT skills over time and adopt more offensive IT strategies. New hacker/terrorist groups may also emerge to compound this problem. Some terrorist networks may even become sophisticated enough to sustain and coordinate offensive campaigns in both the virtual and physical realms. What is certain, however, is that counterterrorism policy will be able to counter the dangers associated with terrorist IT use only if it becomes attuned to the information age.

Counterterrorist policies and tactics could even alter the speed with which terrorists become informatised groups facing a robust counterterrorism campaign may have less time and resources to acquire new technologies. For such reasons, it seems advisable that counterterrorism policymakers and strategists bear in mind the following recommendations.

First, monitor changes in the use of IT by terrorist groups, differentiating between organisational and offensive capabilities. Counterterrorism policies will have to take into account the type of IT capabilities developed by each group, targeting their specific technological vulnerabilities. Evaluating how IT shapes a group's organisational processes and offensive activities will remain a critical component of the threat assessment. Monitoring the shift in capabilities for each type of IT use and then examining trends in the aggregate can also help forecast future terrorist behavior. Among the most significant trends to be carefully examined is the possible emergence of a new, and potentially dangerous, breed of terrorists groups that are highly informatised along both the organisational and offensive axes. In this regard, a number of "signposts" should be identified and tracked.

These would include significant increases in the level of technical expertise of known leaders and their subordinates, increases in the frequency of disruptive attacks, increases in the seizures of IT equipment owned by terrorists, the presence and successful recruiting of "hackers for hire," and the availability of effective and relatively secure off-the-shelf information technologies.

Second, target information flows. Since network designs are inherently information intensive, counterterrorism efforts should target the information flows of netwar groups. Intercepting and monitoring terrorist information exchanges should remain a top priority, and the implementation of "Project Trailblazer" by the National Security Agency to develop a system that can crack new encryption software, fiber-optic cables, and cellular phone transmissions represents a useful addition to America's signals intelligence capability. Equally important, policymakers should consider going beyond the passive monitoring of information flows and toward the active disruption of such communications. To the degree that erroneous or otherwise misleading information is planted into a network's information flows by what are seemingly credible sources, over time the integrity and relevance of the network itself will be compromised. This in turn could breed distrust and further cripple a group's ability to operate in a dispersed and decentralised fashion-essentially eliminating a netwar group's key competitive advantage. Increased emphasis on targeting information flows should not exclude nonelectronic efforts to gather intelligence and undermine the network. Indeed, human intelligence will remain an important tool for intercepting (and injecting) information not transmitted through electronic means of communication. This is an especially pressing concern, given that several intelligence observers have pointed to a lack of U. S. capability in this area.

Third, deter IT-based offensive IO through better infrastructure protection. Changes in the vulnerability of critical infrastructures can significantly alter a terrorist's IT calculus. If such infrastructures, such as those that manage air traffic control, were to become relatively more vulnerable, they might become more attractive as targets: Terrorists could strike at a distance, generating as much—if not more—destruction as would have been caused by the use of traditional weapons.

Fourth, beat networked terrorists at their own game: "It takes networks to fight networks." Governments wishing to counter netwar terrorism will need to adopt organisational designs and strategies like those of their adversaries. This does not mean mirroring the opponent, but rather learning to draw on the same design principles of network forms. These principles depend to some extent upon technological innovation, but mainly on a willingness to innovate organisationally and doctrinally and by building new mechanisms for interagency and multijurisdictional cooperation. The Technical Support Working Group (TSWG) is a good example of a nontraditional government interagency group with more than 100 member organisations from at least 13 federal agencies and a growing number of local and state agencies. Its principal aim is to help develop and deploy technologies to combat terrorism. The information age and the consequent advent of netwar have blurred the boundary between domestic and international threats, as well as between civilian and military threats. This in turn demands greater interagency coordination within the counterterrorism community.

The threat posed by cyber terrorism has grabbed the attention of the mass media, the security community, and the information technology (IT) industry. Journalists, politicians, and experts in a variety of fields have popularised a scenario in which sophisticated cyber terrorists electronically break into computers that control dams or air traffic control systems, wreaking havoc and endangering not only millions of lives but national security itself. Because most critical infrastructure is networked through computers, the potential threat from cyber terrorism is very alarming today. Hackers, although not motivated by the same goals that inspire terrorists, have demonstrated that individuals can gain access to sensitive information and to the operation of crucial services.

Terrorists, at least in theory, could thus follow the hackers' lead and then, having broken into government and private computer systems, cripple or at least disable the military, financial, and service sectors of advanced economies. The growing dependence of our societies on information technology has created a new form of vulnerability, giving terrorists the chance to approach targets that would otherwise be utterly unassailable, such as national defense systems and air traffic control systems. The more technologically developed a country is, the more vulnerable it becomes to cyber attacks against its infrastructure. Concern about the potential danger posed by cyber terrorism is thus well founded. That does not mean, however, that all the fears that have been voiced in the media and in other public forums are rational and reasonable. Some fears are simply unjustified, while others are highly exaggerated. In addition, the distinction between the potential and the actual damage inflicted by cyber terrorists has too often been ignored, and the relatively benign activities of most hackers have been conflated with the specter of pure cyber terrorism.

The energy industry and many other sectors have become potential targets for various cyber disruptions by creating internet links (both physical and wireless) between their networks and supervisory control and data acquisition (SCADA) systems. These SCADA systems manage the flow of electricity and natural gas and control various industrial systems and facilities, including chemical processing plants, water purification and water delivery operations, wastewater management facilities, and a host of manufacturing firms. A terrorist's ability to control, disrupt, or alter the command and monitoring functions performed by these systems could threaten regional and possibly national security.

According to Symantec, one of the world's corporate leaders in the field of cyber security, new vulnerabilities to a cyber attack are being discovered all the time. The company reported that the number of "software holes" (software security flaws that allow malicious hackers to exploit the system) grew by 80 percent in 2002. Still, Symantec claimed that no single cyber terrorist attack was recorded. This may reflect the fact that terrorists do not yet have the required know-how. Alternatively, it may illustrate that hackers are not sympathetic to the goals of terrorist organisations-should the two groups join forces, however, the results could be devastating. Equally alarming is the prospect of terrorists themselves designing computer software for government agencies.

Amid all the dire warnings that the subject of cyber terrorism generates, it is important to remember one simple statistic: so far, there has been no recorded instance of a terrorist cyber attack on public facilities, transportation systems, nuclear power plants, power grids, or other key components of the national infrastructure. Cyber attacks are common, but they have not been conducted by terrorists and they have not sought to inflict the kind of damage that would qualify them as cyber terrorism.

Technological expertise and use of the internet do not constitute evidence of planning for a cyber attack. Neither al Qaeda nor any other terrorist organisation appears to have tried to stage a serious cyber attack. For now, insiders or individual hackers are responsible for most attacks and intrusions and the hackers' motives are not political. According to a report issued in 2002 by IBM Global Security Analysis Lab, 90 percent of hackers are amateurs with limited technical proficiency, 9 percent are more skilled at gaining unauthorised access but do not damage the files they read, and only 1 percent are highly skilled and intent on copying files or damaging programs and systems. Most hackers, it should be noted, try to expose security flaws in computer software, mainly in the operating systems produced by Microsoft. Their efforts in this direction have sometimes embarrassed corporations but have also been responsible for alerting the public and security professionals to serious security flaws. Moreover, although there are hackers with the ability to damage systems, disrupt e-commerce, and force websites offline, the vast majority of hackers do not have the necessary skills and knowledge.

Many computer security experts do not believe that it is possible to use the internet to inflict death on a large scale. Some pointed out that the resilience of computer systems to attack is the result of significant investments of time, money, and expertise. Nuclear weapons systems are protected by "air-gapping": they are not connected to the internet or to any open computer network and thus they cannot be accessed by intruders, terrorists, or hackers. It seems fair to say that the current threat posed by cyber terrorism has been exaggerated.

Cyber terrorism merges two spheres—terrorism and technology—that many people, including most lawmakers and senior administration officials, do not fully understand and therefore tend to fear. Moreover, some groups are eager to exploit this ignorance. Numerous technology companies, still reeling from the collapse of the high-tech bubble, have sought to attract federal research grants by recasting themselves as innovators in computer security and thus vital contributors to national security. Future terrorists may indeed see greater potential for cyber terrorism than do the terrorists of today. The next generation of terrorists is now growing up in a digital world, one in which hacking tools are sure to become more powerful, simpler to use, and easier to access. Cyber terrorism may also become more attractive as the real and virtual worlds become more closely coupled.

6

Combating Cyber Crime

Cyber crime is defined as any criminal activity which uses network access to commit a criminal act. With the exponential growth of Internet connections, the opportunities to exploit weaknesses in Information Security are multiplying. Attacks may be internal or external, with the former being easier to perpetrate. Cyber crime remains a major area of information security risk. The sophistication of these threats is consistently increasing and the methods employed to combat these threats must match this level of sophistication. As a result, it is necessary for all systems users to be especially vigilant at all times.

The growing danger from cyber crimes-harmful acts committed from or against a computer or network-is beginning to claim attention in national capitals. Yet, in most countries, existing laws may be unenforceable against such acts. Outdated laws and regulations, and weak enforcement mechanisms for protecting networked information, create an inhospitable environment in which to conduct e-business within a country and across national boundaries. As e-business expands globally, the need for strong and consistent means to protect networked information will grow. Extending the rule of law into cyberspace is a critical step to create a trustworthy environment for people and businesses.

Because attacks against computers typically do not require the attacker to be physically present at the site of the attack, the risk of being identified is significantly reduced. Besides the technological challenges this presents, the legal issues involved in pursuing and prosecuting intruders adds a layer of difficulty as they cross multiple geographical and legal boundaries. An effective solution can only come in the form of international collaboration. Addressing these vulnerabilities will necessarily require flexible, evolutionary approaches that span both the public and private sectors, and protect both domestic and international security. In the area of law enforcement, the internet constitutes a new patrol area in many respects.

Unlike jurisdictions based on national and political borders, the digital information infrastructure does not have a central location in the physical world. So not only is responding to attacks difficult technically but also many of the accepted methods for practicing law enforcement are ineffective. Recent G8 and OPEC activities are examples of increasing recognition of this international need. Practitioners, researchers, software vendors, and incident response teams realised that aspects of their work that address security flaws to reduce risk to our critical infrastructures might become illegal under the proposed legislation. This was clearly not the original intent of the treaty or the resulting legislation. This is just one example of the urgent need for ongoing communication among policymakers, technologists, and others to ensure that future policies and agreements on a national and international scale are practical and effective.

Information exchange and interaction among many parties is paramount to producing comprehensive and practical approaches and solutions to the complex problems faced. Simply bringing parties together is not enough. We need to consider the issues that must be addressed to support a global incident response effort and to reduce the likelihood, number, and extent of computer security incidents. Many network protocols that now form part of the information infrastructure were designed without computer security in mind. Without a secure infrastructure, it is difficult to avoid security problems and resolve computer security incidents.

The combination of rapidly changing technology, rapidly expanding use, and new, often unimagined uses of the information infrastructure creates a volatile situation in which the nature of threats and vulnerabilities is difficult to assess and even more difficult to predict. It is inexpensive, quick, and easy for anyone to launch attacks against our critical information infrastructures. Conversely, it is expensive, longterm and complex to take the steps needed to harden the information infrastructure to make it less susceptible to attack, and to enable us to respond more effectively and efficiently when attacks do happen. Incident response and computer security teams consist of practitioners and technologists who have a wealth of operational experience but lack authority to make policy and security decisions in their organisations. They also may have limited funding and lack professional recognition. This has negative consequences; a given team"s organisation may not allow enough staff to respond effectively to security incidents. Similarly, a team may not have sufficient authority to influence and ensure improved computer security and comprehensive response. Moreover, at this time, there is no infrastructure to support a coordinated global incident response effort, although there are a few components in place that can form the basis of this infrastructure.

A variety of issues must be addressed when considering how to promote an effective global incident response infrastructure. These include discussions about which organisations will coordinate and participate in the development effort, how current groups and forums can fit their mission and objectives into an agenda to create a global infrastructure, and what possible structures and mechanisms might be required and effective in the future. The Melissa Virus attack underscores the lack of such a global response structure for incident response. Because individual teams focused on their individual or national response needs, there was no operational global response effort. To handling the computer security problems, a global role for the incident response and security teams is necessary. These teams should use the strength of their technical coordination today to link to the international organisations aimed at tracking trends and activity of cyber crime and terrorist groups.

International Coordination against Cyber Crime

Computer security incidents are reported to regional or national response teams. Frequently these reports are motivated by a desire to patch any vulnerabilities that were used to enable the attack and not by a desire to determine either the international scope or uncover the intruder. An exception is when the target is a government or other potentially sensitive site where the response depends on knowing the origin of the attack. In this case, the tracking of the individual is frequently turned over to the foreign office or other international relations office for the coordination necessary to track the intruder. Information communicated in computer security incidents is controlled by the direct participation of the regions involved in the incident.

Frequently information is reported to incident response teams where there is not a specific victim or computer security incident but rather an indication that some activity may be ongoing in some other part of the community. There is currently no standard way of sharing that information, although sometimes this information is posted to a shared list of FIRST members. This is one of the main areas that needs drastic improvement in the future in order to effectively process cyber crime and terrorist indicators that may be detected within the incident response community.

One significant problem with the tracking of malicious activity to its origin is that it requires the cooperation of many independent administrative domains operating internationally. This makes the creation of a universally acceptable technology solution unlikely. Thus a reasonable approach to track and trace today is the combination of technically experienced personnel working with these administrative domains to gain their cooperation voluntarily to trace back malicious activity to the actual threat behind the activity. With the volume of information gathered by the CERT/CC and other international response teams, it is likely that the network of these incident response teams will provide the best start to tracking the activity of intruders and other malicious cyber activity to determine the point of origin.

While this can never be a guaranteed activity, putting together all of the international evidence related to a malicious activity will provide the best cyber evidence of this point of origin and perhaps help to distinguish between domestic and international threats. In addition to the information gathered by incident response teams, the CERT/CC has a unique relationship with many of the Internet Service Providers (ISPs) and network operation centers that enable the CERT/CC to work with both victims and transport providers to track specific activity to its immediate point of origin. Then with its reputation of impartiality, the CERT/CC can frequently work with the administrators of these sites to trace back the activity one step further to attempt to find the true place of origin.

There is an urgent and ongoing need to provide a global infrastructure to provide a fast, effective, and comprehensive response to computer security incidents on a local, national, and international scale. At this time, there is no infrastructure to support a coordinated global incident response effort. The need for an international forum to respond to computer security incidents was recognised in the early 1990s and resulted in the formation of FIRST (Forum of Incident Response and Security Teams).

Today, FIRST consists of more than 80 incident response and security teams from 19 countries and provides a closed forum for these teams to share experiences, exchange information related to incidents, and to promote preventive activities. Although other teams exist that are not yet FIRST members and new teams are continuously being established, for years to come there will not be enough teams to address the growing need for global incident response. Additionally, FIRST as it exists today is a voluntary organisation with no operational element. As such, it provides an introduction service and meeting place for teams to establish trusted interactions, but it is not currently able to provide the necessary coordinated global effort or meet other needs, such as a more open flow of sensitive information and close collaboration to respond to widespread events. Among the challenges to expanding the role of FIRST are lack of appropriate policies and procedures, lack of formal agreements, and the difficulty of gaining entry into the incident response community.

– *Establishing policies and procedures.* The pioneer computer security incident response teams, formed in the late 1980s, were faced with defining their own appropriate operational guidelines with little or no experience on which to draw from. It has taken years for these now-established teams to develop comprehensive policies and procedures for their internal operations. Today, newly forming teams are not much better off than the early pioneers were, as little documented guidance is available. Moreover, this same community as a whole is still sorely lacking in the area of policies and procedures to support operations among teams. The progress being made in this area is limited and slow. It is mostly limited to a few isolated groups of incident response teams who work together regularly and have a business need to reach agreement. Progress typically comes to a halt when teams become overwhelmed by the number of issues that need to be addressed before they can reach agreement-such as no common agreement on terminology, definitions, and priorities.

Forming cooperative relationships among teams. Currently, many teams agree to cooperate based on trust alone; they have no supporting contractual agreements to provide the foundation for their interactions. In fact, it is even more complex than that, as in some cases trust has been developed between individuals from given teams. So when trusted individuals leave those teams, the trust relationship may go with them. This can potentially result in the isolation of teams that were once part of a cooperative incident response community. Additionally, the information communicated between two teams during an incident is not well defined. The extent of the information might depend on who is involved, their experience with the other team involved, and the specific staff members who are interacting.

A global incident response infrastructure would be the most effective way to facilitate response and to ensure that information is exchanged securely. This approach helps to ensure that response is effective, reliable, and timely. Information exchange and interaction among entities is paramount to producing comprehensive and practical approaches and solutions to the complex problems faced. Again, bringing parties together is not enough. We need to consider the issues that must be addressed to support a global incident response effort and to reduce the likelihood, number, and extent of computer security incidents.

Global Infrastructure for Incident Response

Some of the possible models for implementing a global infrastructure for incident response are described below:

1. A global coordination center
2. International time zone coordination centers
3. National coordination centers.

Global Coordination Center

A natural model to consider is the establishment of a single center to coordinate global response to computer security incidents. At least a two-level hierarchy would be established, with the global coordination center at the top level and the rest of the infrastructure at one or more lower levels. While conceptually this sounds like a clean and simple approach, it is fraught with practical and political issues. We will only address here what we consider main "show-stopper" issues. Experience has shown that it is insufficient to designate a component of the incident response infrastructure and expect it to succeed. To be successful, a component must gain constituency, recognition, and trust. It is unlikely that any one organisation (of any form) could be established that could gain the global recognition and trust of every nation in the world. As a result, a single organisation providing a truly global coordination service is not a viable option.

International Time Zone Coordination Centers

Another frequently discussed model is the establishment of a number of international coordination centers located in different time zones around the world to coordinate response to computer security incidents around the globe. If these centers were run by a single organisation, the result would be the same as the global coordination center. So this model needs to be viewed from a different perspective.

The centers would act as peers and coordinate their efforts, but each would be separately operated and run. This also would result in at least a two-level hierarchy being established, with the international coordination centers at the top level and the rest of the infrastructure at one or more lower levels. The community has some practical experience in establishing, funding, and operating such centers both in the USA (the CERT/CC coordination role) and in Europe (the EuroCERT coordination role). The discussion of the issues below are based on lessons learned from those experiences. The role is one of coordination in response to incidents and events and not one of operationally handling incident and events.

National teams have resisted the suggestion that a coordination team for a continent might take over the operational mission for a region. They believe that the operations should stay within the team, close to the constituency, where the funding is and where the language, culture, and laws are understood. However, in some instances national funding bodies have given funding to EuroCERT instead of to the national team, falsely believing the international coordination entity would be a substitute for any national incident handling effort. The impetus for a European coordination center resulted from the recognition that limited coordination among European teams was taking place and also from a general feeling that a coordination center located in Europe was needed for practical reasons.

Although it is possible to provide an operational incident response service on a national or international basis, provision of a multinational or global operational service has so far been unsuccessful. The reasons for this include the following:

- *Funding.* Nations fail to recognise the need to fund both a national service and an international one. The funding source of an incident response team has great influence on how that team will be perceived and trusted both nationally and internationally.
- *Authority and balance of power.* Nations want to be responsible for their own needs and do not necessarily want a coordination center for the continent becoming privy to their data. Additionally, hostility between nations in the same geographical region will inhibit or prohibit cooperation. The role of a continental coordination center brings responsibility, prestige, and recognition. As a result, many countries may want to take on the role, making it hard to reach agreement. As previously discussed, trust and respect must be earned; they cannot be designated or delegated. There must be consensus and buy-in on the location and host of the continental coordination center.
- *Issues of scale.* Organisations have yet to address the practicalities of scale when trying to dig through a huge volume of data resulting from a global influx of information. When providing coverage for more than

one country, cultural and language issues come into play. In the incident response field, it is vital to ensure that all parties involved understand what is being communicated. It is unreasonable to expect that each international coordination center would hand off coordination responsibility for activities relating to its constituency to another international coordination center. As a result, to be effective, each international coordination center would need to provide a basic level of services on a 24/7 basis. There are a number of practical issues that must be addressed when dealing with multiple time zones. It is hard to transition work from one time zone to another as the day passes around the world. Such transition will invariably result in loss of both continuity and productivity due to any "rampup" during the hand-off.

National Coordination Centers

The number of national teams is continuing to increase, and many other existing and newly forming teams have constituencies that fall within national boundaries. National boundaries provide a demarcation for policies, procedures, and jurisdiction for information exchange; thus, they provide an excellent opportunity for coordinating on a national level. This approach is based on having every nation establish a national coordination center. This model is not as clean an approach as the first two and has its own limitations, but it has more potential to achieve global coverage. Although these components need only provide a coordination effort, the centers might also undertake an operational incident-handling role, depending on the size of the nations involved. One limitation of this approach is that there are teams (other than international coordination centers) that provide services to constituencies that cross national boundaries (incident response teams for multinational corporations). For this and other reasons, it makes sense to consider additional coordination boundaries to support such cases; coordinating centers might exist for teams with similar needs, such as those within the banking or telecomm communities. This would result in at least a three-level hierarchy. This hierarchy could be made flexible enough to enable teams, as appropriate, to be served directly by a coordination center without the need for national coordination. Issues to be addressed within this model include the following:

- *Funding sources.* Funding will come from different sources and will be dependent on the function provided by the team, the constituency served, and the team"s position in the hierarchy. Participating teams will need to seek their own funding sources to support them as an infrastructure component. There is potential for funding from role two to provide support for infrastructure components to conduct sensitive/closed discussions. From an operational perspective, it would be possible to seek funding for groups of infrastructure components to collaborate and to provide funding for national/multinational organisations to develop tools and services to support the infrastructure.

- *Authority and balance of power.* Determining how to appropriately position a given team in the hierarchy can be addressed by a combination of approaches. In some cases, this will occur bottom-up because there will be components that do not wish to provide the funding to perform a coordination role. Some teams that gain the trust and respect of others may naturally find themselves being recognised in a coordination role. In other cases, the level in the hierarchy will result from existing organisational structures.

However, recognition of national teams themselves will result not only from national designation, but also from international recognition. Until base standards are recognised in this area, the situation will remain complex and problematic. Many existing "national" teams are not truly national because their constituencies do not officially extend to a nation but, instead, to national academic and research networks. A neutral arbitration service will be necessary for the discussion and resolution of disputes between incident response teams at all levels. We suggest that this service be provided by the professional society component of role two.

– *Issues of scale* . For large-scale events that affect a significant number of sites across the world, this approach can become complex without a single team taking on the coordination effort for the event. Agreeing to allocate the coordination role "on the fly" would not be productive or efficient. It might be appropriate to identify and recognise a number of teams that are willing and able to take on such a role in advance.

– *Organisational requirements.* With such a large number of nations around the globe, a higher tier of coordinating teams will need to exist for this approach to work effectively. This higher tier is likely to evolve from a limited number of international coordination centers becoming established for small groups of cooperating nations and other coordination centers representing specific interest groups and industries. In reality, we will have a web of incident response teams that have the flexibility of coordination on a number of levels.

JURISDICTIONAL CRITERIA

Currently, the volume of cross-boarder computer has increased significantly. Currently, whole sectors of economy, such as banking and international aviation, rely heavily or even exclusively on international telecommunication networks. With the continuing development of standards and norms for electronic data interchange (EDI), such as that under the auspices of the United Nation Electronic Data Interchange for Administration, Commerce and Transportation (UN/EDIFACT), the use of EDI will increase substantially in the decade to come.

The international element in the commission of computer crime create new problems and challenges for the law. Systems may be accessed in one country, the date manipulate in another and the consequences felt in a third country. Hackers can operate physically operate in one country, move electronically across the world from one network to another and easily access databases on a different continent. The result of this ability is that different sovereignties, jurisdictions, laws and rules will come into play. More than in any other transnational crime, the speed, mobility, flexibility, significance and value of electronic transactions profoundly challenge the existing rules of international crime law.

Countering computer crimes committed from a distance and having and increasing range of international targets will require a well-developed network of inter-State cooperation to attain effective investigation and prosecution. In the light of the technicalities of international interaction, cooperation between nations in criminal matters is crucial. These issues have to be addressed by all countries, whether they be producers, users or consumers of the new information technologies, since these technologies ate becoming an integral part of economic, social and culture development.

In seeking solutions to the above problems, the international community should strive for the following:

1. Maximising cooperation between nations in order to address, firstly, the potential for enormous economic losses and, secondly, the general threat to privacy and other fundamental values that near-instantaneous cross-border electronic transactions may create;
2. Worldwide protection so as to avoid "data paradises" or computer crimes havens where computer criminals can find refuge or launch there attacks;
3. A lawfully structured cooperation scheme, taking into account and balancing the necessities of international trade and relations on the one hand and the rights and freedoms of the individual on the other hand.

There are a number of problems related to the issue of jurisdiction. In every computer crime, the determination of the locus delicti (the location of the offence) will affect the ability of a particular country to sanction the crime. Will the sanction arise by virtue of territorial jurisdiction and domestic law, or must extraterritorial principles apply? Today, it is technologically possible for an operator to punch a keyboard in country A so as to modify data tored in country B, even the operator does not know that the ata are stored there, to have the modified data transferred over telecommunications network through several other countries, and cause an outcome in country C. On the basis of the physical ct, the technical modification, the transmission of the alsified data and the consequences, three or perhaps more ountries will have been involved and may have a claim to urisdictional competency.

Depending on which elements or stages of the crime are given priority, several countries in the above scenario could, within their full sovereignty, declare the incident as having occurred on their territory, thus invoking the principle of territorial jurisdiction in order to prosecute and sanction. This raises a potential jurisdictional conflict, as well as the question of the appropriate arbitration of these equal claim for jurisdiction, the applicability of the non bis in idem rule, and the impact of the lex mitior rule.

The recurring threat of computer viruses worms in another striking example of transnationality. If a virus infects the system in one location, the infection can spread with destructive rapidity and affect programmes throughout the international network. What criteria should apply in determining which country may act? Once again, several choices are available: the country in which the virus was introduced, all countries in which software or databases were affected and all countries in which results were felt. It is possible that it may not manifest itself far away from the country of origin. It is also possible that it may not manifest itself until considerable time has passed, when retracing the technological path of the of the original offender has become difficult, as, for example, in cases of the so-called time-bomb virus. What, then, determines the competency to prosecute and sanction? Can it be the best evidence rule or the first-come, first-served principle, or do the traditional solutions discussed below still stand firm?

The primacy of the principle of territoriality is generally accepted in sphere of criminal jurisdiction. The principle is based on mutual respect of sovereign equality between States and is linked with the principle of non-intervention in the affairs and exclusive domain of other States. Even in the exceptional event that a country might apply extraterritorial jurisdiction for a sake of protecting its own vital interests, the primacy of the extraterritorial principle is not altered.

The ubiquity doctrine is often referred to in determining the place of commission. The offence will be considered to have been committed in its entirety within a country"s jurisdiction if one of the constitutive elements of the offence, or the ultimate result, occurred within that country"s borders. Jurisdiction is equally applicable to co-perpetrators and accomplices. Common law countries also use the effects doctrine in addition to focusing on the physical act. This doctrine locates crimes in the territory in which the crime is intended to produce, or actually does produce, its effects. Thus, where various elements or effects of a crime may occur in more than one country, the two doctrines of territorial jurisdiction may lead to concurrent, legitimate jurisdictional claims. These positive conflicts of jurisdiction, while at first glance not very problematic in determining the appropriate judicial response, do contain some inherent risks. The most fundamental problem is the general refusal, particularly in civil law systems, to apply the double jeopardy rule. Thus, the accused is submitted to a multitude of prosecutions for the same act.

Equally important is the manner of classification of the multiple acts potentially involved in a pattern of computer crimes. In particular, in cases of repeated data manipulation, data espionage or unauthorised access, it is unclear whether the acts should be considered as separate crimes or as a single act by application of the principle of international connexity, by which a single prosecution for the whole transaction would be justified. States should, therefore, endeavour to negotiate agreements on the positive conflicts issue. These agreements should address the following issues:

1. An explicit priority of jurisdictional criteria: for example, of location of act over location of effect, of

the place of physical detainment of the suspect over in absentia proceedings or extradition;

2. A mechanism for consultation between the States concerned in order to agree upon either the priority of jurisdiction over the offence or the division of the offence into separate acts;
3. Cooperation in the investigation, prosecution and punishment of international computer offences, including the admissibility of evidence lawfully gathered in the other countries, and the recognition of punishment effectively served in other jurisdictions. This would prevent unreasonable hardship to the accused, otherwise possible by an inflexible interpretation of the territoriality principle.

The issue of international computer crime also requires an analysis of the principles of extraterritorial jurisdiction. State practice discerns the following theoretical grounds:

1. The active nationality principle, which is based on the nationality of the accused. The principle, when applied in conjunction with the territoriality principle, may result in parallel concurrent jurisdictions, creating a situation of double jeopardy. The use of the active nationality principle is therefore generally confined to serious offences;
2. The passive personality principle, which is based on the nationality of the victims. This principle has been highly criticised, since it could subject a national of State A, although acting lawfully in State A, to punishment in State B for acts done in State A to a national of State B, if the acts were unlawful in State B and State B were to apply the principle. On practice, therefore, this principle is seldom used;
3. The protective principle, which is based on the protection of the vital interests of a State. By this

principle, a State may exercise jurisdiction over foreigners who commit acts that are considered to be a threat to national security. Given the potential for abuse of this principle if security is interpreted too broadly, the protective principle is not highly favoured; in practice, therefore, it is often linked to other doctrines, such as the personality principle or the effects doctrine;

4. The universality principle, based on the protection of universal values. It is usually effected on the basis of express treaty provisions but is otherwise rarely used. It is generally held that this principle should apply only in cases where the crime is serious, where the State that would have jurisdiction over the offence, based on the usual jurisdictional principles, is unable or unwilling to prosecute.

There are no rules of international law, other than the principles of comity and non-intervention, that impose express limitations on the freedom of sovereign States in establishing extraterritorial criminal jurisdiction. Where there is strong international solidarity by way of customary or conventional international law, jurisdiction over important offences may be decided by the principle of universality, in addition to the applicability of other grounds of jurisdiction. No such conventions exist yet in relation to computer crime. Eventually, however, as has been the case in other major international crimes, international conventions will regulate this area. A spirit of moderation might be expected from States in exercising these jurisdictional principles, in order to encourage international cooperation and to avoid significant conflicts of jurisdiction with other States. In that spirit, the passive personality principle, although sometimes used to protect the economic interests of nationals, is highly disputed, while universality is best limited to express treaty provisions. The protective principle may be relevant for certain types of computer offences, because it grants jurisdiction to a State over offences committed outside its territory, in the defence of fundamental (vital) interests.

There exists very little consensus on what constitutes vital interests. No doubt a sovereign State might consider attacks on data or telecommunication infrastructures, when related to basic government activities (police data, military data, State security systems etc.), to fall within its purview. However, a tendency may arise to consider certain economic interests, naturally involving a significant amount of transborder data flow, as a vital concern of the State. Nevertheless, caution is needed in regard to such extensions, since they can affect adversely the legitimate flow of information and data, as well as other economic and social interests.

Therefore, the State concerned should be expected to take due account of the principles of cooperation, comity and reasonableness, which should govern State action in exercising extraterritorial jurisdiction. Even if very few specific computer-related concerns seem apparent, the general issues in extraterritorial jurisdiction remain valid: the need for harmonised legislation, the settlement of concurrent jurisdictional claims, the international validity of the non bis idem principle and the development of agreements on mutual cooperation and the transfer of criminal proceedings.

Computer Data Banks

Within the international economic environment, in particular within multinational corporate structures, data are often stored centrally in one country, with on-line access available to company partners operating in the territory of other countries.Criminal investigations in such situations are presented with the problem of how to retrieve the data, as potential evidence, that are stored abroad, when investigating by means of on-line access to that data. The question arises whether the investigating authorities may penetrate the database by direct access, without the intervention, knowledge or agreement of the State in which the data are located.

Urgent situations compelling the preservation of evidence may require that data be made readily available or, at least, that they be seized and blocked, thereby securing their evidential value. A suspect with sufficient speed and expertise in the access to and the functioning of the system could otherwise interfere with the data and make them unavailable by, for example, erasing them or transmitting them to another data bank. Traditional means for cooperation between States in criminal cases do exist, in the form of conventional mutual assistance agreements, particularly the procedure of the letters rogatory. This procedure, however, by which a State is requested to undertake an investigation on its own territory on behalf of the investigating State, is highly time-consuming.

The investigation of crime in the computer environment requires quicker, more efficient action. Another problem arises when a person, natural or legal, is compelled by the investigating State to produce data located in another State, whether or not they are available by on-line access, even though under the law of the State of storage that person is obliged to secrecy. There is no unanimity today on the solution to these problems. However, the view that the deliberate investigation of on-line data constitutes a violation of the sovereignty of the other State is probably correct, whether it is done by the investigating authorities from the premises of the suspect or from their own terminals. In fact, such access might even be considered in the other State as a form of computer crime, such as unauthorised access.

The only explicit rule in international public law relevant to this situation seems to be the non-intervention principle, which historically has been applied only when foreign agents have operated physically on a State"s territory. Nevertheless, the direct penetration of data banks appears very similar to acts of physical intervention by official foreign agents. The analogy is strengthened if the acts of penetration also constitute an offence in the other State. However, some people will probably resist the analogy and accept the legality of this penetration.There is a definite need to address these questions, which are indeed not hypothetical ones, and to find solutions that balance the requirement of quick action with the appropriate respect for the sovereign rights of the other State in matters of police or investigatory action within its territory. States could, therefore, strive to conclude agreements that make direct penetration acceptable only as an exception.

The problem of on-line transborder searches of computerised data has not been adequately addressed so far. By virtue of not being cooperative acts, such actions do not fall within the traditional category of mutual assistance in criminal matters. However, the appropriate solution is not to view States as having a complete unilateral freedom to act, provided there is no violation of the non-intervention principle by physical interference.

Addressing Transnational Computer Crime

Transnational computer crime can be efficiently addressed only if the countries involved agree to provide maximum cooperation in countering it. This cooperation is usually organised by multi- or bilateral conventions may given rise to a number of problems of which States should be aware.

First, as for other forms of international cooperation, the requirement of dual criminality may be an issue.

Refusal of assistance could be based on the ground that the act in relation to which the request is made is not an offence in the territory of the requested State. Thus there is a clear need to make the substantive criminal law of computer crime correspond from State to State. Even if the dual criminality rule is not an aspect of all incidents of mutual assistance, it is often a requirement in cases of search and seizure, which is a particularly important means of assistance where data are concerned. Double criminality, furthermore, is basic to other common cooperation modes, such as extradition, or other schemes for solving jurisdictional conflicts. Unless domestic criminal legislation, as it develops, moves beyond xpressions of sovereignty to espousing common principles as greed among nations, conflicts will not be avoided. Efforts by tates to harmonise their domestic laws will prevent conflicts of urisdiction and, at minimum will lay the basic groundwork for ooperation. It is, therefore, imperative that States undertake action to achieve this aim. Such action may range from the undertaking of consultations among States prior to enacting domestic legislation; solutions for harmonisation, such as recommended guidelines for national legislation; and the elaboration of a convention of substantive law that defines computer crime under international law, including the governing principles in jurisdiction and cooperation.

Secondly, a form of mutual assistance rendered to requesting States is the search and seizure of data banks or carriers that store or transmit information. The target of request is not the carrier itself but the intangible specific data. If seizure remains applicable only to physical objects, the carrier is still at issue. The technical storage capacity of such data banks and carriers often far exceeds the volume of content requested by the investigating State. Explicit rules should be elaborated in relation to the surplus of information a data bank or carrier might contain, which would allow the execution of letters rogatorys upon only the targeted data. Notions such as relevance, proportionality and defined purpose should necessarily be included.

The third concern relates to potential grounds of refusal, which almost uniformly include the protection of the essential interests of the requested party. Data that relate to the privacy of nationals, including, for example, financial or medical information, could be considered sufficiently sensitive by a State, in its role of protecting its citizens, to be an essential interest. Many computer-related investigations may concern tax fraud or violations of customs, import and export rules, equally subject to the essential public interest qualification.

Given the potential for multiple territorial and extraterritorial jurisdictions, resolving the resulting jurisdictional conflicts will often require an agreement between States. It is therefore possible that the effective exercise of an agreed jurisdiction will involve extradition, since the State of physical location of the suspect may not necessarily be the appropriate forum for prosecuting the crime.

The terms of traditional extradition treaties will remain applicable. Computer crimes do not appear to raise any specific difficulties, provided the requirements of the extradition law and/or treaty are met. The most important issues are the requirement, again, of double criminality, i.e. the impugned conduct would be an offence punishable under the law of both the requesting and the requested State, and the fulfilling of any other conditions that would include computer crime within the category of extraditable offences. This could be accomplished either by setting sanctions for the open formula, e.g. a maximum punishment of a certain number of months, or by including computer crime in the enumerated list of extradition crimes appended to the extradition treaty in question.

Both conditions require careful attention in the computer crime area. The first condition highlights once again the absolute need to legislate the substantive law in each State as consistently as possible, thus avoiding loopholes or conflicting interpretations of the requirements of criminality. The second condition, the extraditable character of the offence, requires an attentive legislative drafting policy. In particular, offences such as unauthorised access to computers or telecommunications facilities are often characterised as minor offences, and penalty scales may not meet the minimum threshold standards of extraditable crimes.

Unfortunately, experience shows that transborder hacking cases are common, significantly affecting important transnational economic networks. It might be advisable to consider serious penalties, at least in cases where the hacking affects the international relations of the victim, whether the victim is a legal or physical person or a State. Disregarding the use of extradition or other cooperation methods could seriously hinder the efficiency of the cooperative response to this important and disturbing phenomenon.

7

Information Technology Act, 2000

The following Act of Parliament received the assent of the President on the 9th of June, 2000, and is hereby published for general information:

THE INFORMATION TECHNOLOGY ACT, 2000
(NO. 21 OF 2000) [9TH JUNE, 2000]

An Act to provide legal recognition for transactions carried out by means of electronic data interchange and other means of electronic communication, commonly referred to as "electronic commerce", which involve the use of alternatives to paper-based methods of communication and storage of information, to facilitate electronic filing of documents with the Government agencies and further to amend the Indian Penal Code, the Indian Evidence Act, 1872, the Bankers' Books Evidence Act, 1891 and the Reserve Bank of India Act, 1934 and for matters connected therewith or incidental thereto:

whereas the General Assembly of the United Nations by resolution A/RES/51/162, dated the 30th January, 1997 has adopted the Model Law on Electronic Commerce adopted by the United Nations Commission on International Trade Law;

and whereas the said resolution recommends *inter alia* that all States give favourable consideration to the said Model Law when they enact or revise their laws, in view of the need for uniformity of the law applicable to alternatives to paper-cased methods of communication and storage of information;

and whereas it is considered necessary to give effect to the said resolution and to promote efficient delivery of Government services by means of reliable electronic records.

be it enacted by Parliament in the Fifty-first Year of the Republic of India as follows:

Chapter I

Preliminary

1. Short title, extent, commencement and application

1) This Act may be called the Information Technology Act, 2000.

2) It shall extend to the whole of India and, save as otherwise provided in this Act, it applies also to any offence or contravention thereunder committed outside India by any person.

3) It shall come into force on such date as the Central Government may, by notification, appoint and different dates may be appointed for different provisions of this Act and any reference in any such provision to the commencement of this Act shall be construed as a reference to the commencement of that provision.

4) Nothing in this Act shall apply to:

   a) a negotiable instrument as defined in section 13 of the Negotiable Instruments Act, 1881;

b) a power-of-attorney as defined in section 1A of the Powers-of-Attorney Act, 1882;

c) a trust as defined in section 3 of the Indian Trusts Act, 1882;

d) a will as defined in clause (h) of section 2 of the Indian Succession Act, 1925 including any other testa-mentary disposition by whatever name called;

e) any contract for the sale or conveyance of immovable property or any interest in such property;

f) any such class of documents or transactions as may be notified by the Central Government in the Official Gazette.

2. Definitions

1) In this Act, unless the context otherwise requires:

a) "access" with its grammatical variations and cognate expressions means gaining entry into, instructing or communicating with the logical, arithmetical, or memory function resources of a computer, computer system or computer network;

b) "addressee" means a person who is intended by the originator to receive the electronic record but does not include any intermediary;

c) "adjudicating officer" means an adjudicating officer appointed under subsection (1) of section 46;

d) "affixing digital signature" with its grammatical variations and cognate expressions means adoption of any methodology or procedure by a person for the purpose of authenticating an electronic record by means of digital signature;

e) "appropriate Government" means as respects any matter:

   i) Enumerated in List II of the Seventh Schedule to the Constitution;

   ii) relating to any State law enacted under List III of the Seventh Schedule to the Constitution, the State Government and in any other case, the Central Government;

f) "asymmetric crypto system" means a system of a secure key pair consisting of a private key for creating a digital signature and a public key to verify the digital signature;

g) "Certifying Authority" means a person who has been granted a licence to issue a Digital Signature Certificate under section 24;

h) "certification practice statement" means a statement issued by a Certifying Authority to specify the practices that the Certifying Authority employs in issuing Digital Signature Certificates;

i) "computer" means any electronic magnetic, optical or other high-speed data processing device or system which performs logical, arithmetic, and memory functions by manipulations of electronic, magnetic or optical impulses, and includes all input, output, processing, storage, computer software, or communi-cation facilities which are connected or related to the computer in a computer system or computer network;

j) "computer network" means the interconnection of one or more computers through

   i) the use of satellite, microwave, terrestrial line or other communication media; and

ii) terminals or a complex consisting of two or more interconnected computers whether or not the interconnection is continuously maintained;

k) "computer resource" means computer, computer system, computer network, data, computer database or software;

l) "computer system" means a device or collection of devices, including input and output support devices and excluding calculators which are not programm-able and capable of being used in conjunction with external files, which contain computer programmes, electronic instructions, input data and output data, that performs logic, arithmetic, data storage and retrieval, communication control and other functions;

m) "Controller" means the Controller of Certifying Authorities appointed under sub-section (1) of section 17;

n) "Cyber Appellate Tribunal" means the Cyber Regulations Appellate Tribunal established under sub-section (1) of section 48;

o) "data" means a representation of information, knowledge, facts, concepts or instructions which are being prepared or have been prepared in a formalised manner, and is intended to be processed, is being processed or has been processed in a computer system or computer network, and may be in any form (including computer printouts magnetic or optical storage media, punched cards, punched tapes) or stored internally in the memory of the computer;

p) "digital signature" means authentication of any electronic record by a subscriber by means of an electronic method or procedure in accordance with the provisions of section 3;

q) "Digital Signature Certificate" means a Digital Signature Certificate issued under sub-section (4) of section 35;

r) "electronic form" with reference to information means any information generated, sent, received or stored in ,media, magnetic, optical, computer memory, micro film, computer generated microfiche or similar device;

s) "Electronic Gazette" means the Official Gazette published in the electronic form;

t) "electronic record" means data, record or data generated, image or sound stored, received or sent in an electronic form or microfilm or computer generated microfiche;

u) "function", in relation to a computer, includes logic, control arithmetical process, deletion, storage and retrieval and communication or telecommunication from or within a computer;

v) "information" includes data, text, images, sound, voice, codes, computer programmes, software and databases or microfilm or computer generated micro-fiche:

w) "intermediary" with respect to any particular electronic message means any person who on behalf of another person receives, stores or transmits that message or provides any service with respect to that message;

x) "key pair", in an asymmetric crypto system, means a private key and its mathematically related public key, which are so related that the public key can verify a digital signature created by the private key;

y) "law" includes any Act of Parliament or of a State Legislature, Ordinances promulgated by the President or a Governor, as the case may be. Regulations made by the President under Article 240, Bills enacted as President's Act under sub-clause (a) of clause (1) of Article 357 of the Constitution and includes rules, regulations, bye-laws and orders issued or made thereunder;

z) "licence" means a licence granted to a Certifying Authority under section 24;

za) "originator" means a person who sends, generates, stores or transmits any electronic message or causes any electronic message to be sent, generated, stored or transmitted to any other person but does not include an inter-mediary;

zb) "prescribed" means prescribed by rules made under this Act;

zc) "private key" means the key of a key pair used to create a digital signature;

zd) "public key" means the key of a key pair used to verify a digital signature and listed in the Digital Signature Certificate;

ze) "secure system" means computer hardware, software, and procedure that:

a) are reasonably secure from unauthorised access and misuse;

b) provide a reasonable level of reliability and correct operation;

c) are reasonably suited to performing the intended functions; and

d) adhere to generally accepted security procedures;

zf) "security procedure" means the security procedure prescribed under section 16 by the Central Government;

zg) "subscriber" means a person in whose name the Digital Signature Certificate is issued;

zh) "verify" in relation to a digital signature, electronic record or public key, with its grammatical variations and cognate expressions means to determine whether

a) the initial electronic record was affixed with the digital signature by the use of private key corresponding to the public key of the subscriber;

b) the initial electronic record is retained intact or has been altered since such electronic record was so affixed with the digital signature.

2) Any reference in this Act to any enactment or any provision thereof shall, in relation to an area in which such enactment or such provision is not in force, be construed as a reference to the corresponding law or the relevant provision of the corresponding law, if any, in force in that area.

CHAPTER II

DIGITAL SIGNATURE

3. Authentication of electronic records

1) Subject to the provisions of this section any subscriber may authenticate an electronic record by affixing his digital signature.

2) The authentication of the electronic record shall be effected by the use of asymmetric crypto system and hash function which envelop and transform the initial electronic record into another electronic record.

   Explanation: For the purposes of this sub-section, "hash function" means an algorithm mapping or translation of one sequence of bits into another, generally smaller, set known as "hash result" such that an electronic record yields the same hash result every time the algorithm is executed with the same electronic record as its input making it computationally infeasible

   a) to derive or reconstruct the original electronic record from the hash result produced by the algorithm;

   b) that two electronic records can produce the same hash result using the algorithm.

3) Any person by the use of a public key of the subscriber can verify the electronic record.

4) The private key and the public key are unique to the subscriber and constitute a functioning key pair.

CHAPTER III

ELECTRONIC GOVERNANCE

4. Legal recognition of electronic records

Where any law provides that information or any other matter shall be in writing or in the typewritten or printed form, then, notwithstanding anything contained in such law, such requirement shall be deemed to have been satisfied if such information or matter is:

a) rendered or made available in an electronic form; and

b) accessible so as to be usable for a subsequent reference.

5. Legal recognition of digital signatures

Where any law provides that information or any other matter shall be authenticated by affixing the signature or any document shall be signed or bear the signature of any person, then, notwithstanding anything contained in such law, such requirement shall be deemed to have been satisfied, if such information or matter is authenticated by means of digital signature affixed in such manner as may be prescribed by the Central Government.

Explanation: For the purposes of this section, "signed", with its grammatical variations and cognate expressions, shall, with reference to a person, mean affixing of his handwritten signature or any mark on any document and the expression "signature" shall be construed accordingly.

6. Use of electronic records and digital signatures in government and its agencies

1) Where any law provides for

    a) the filing of any form application or any other document with any office, authority, body or agency owned or controlled by the appropriate Government in a particular manner;

    b) the issue or grant of any licence, permit, sanction or approval by whatever name called in a particular manner;

    c) the receipt or payment of money in a particular manner, then, notwithstanding anything contained in any other law for the time being in force, such requirement shall be deemed to have been satisfied if such filing, issue, grant, receipt or payment, as the case may be, is effected by means of such electronic form as may be prescribed by the appropriate Government.

2) The appropriate Government may, for the purposes of sub-section (1), by rules, prescribe:

   a) the manner and format in which such electronic records shall be filed, created or issued;

   b) the manner or method of payment of any fee or charges for filing, creation or issue any electronic record under clause (a).

7. Retention of electronic records

1) Where any law provides that documents, records or information shall be retained for any specific period, then, that requirement shall be deemed to have been satisfied if such documents, records or information are retained in the electronic form, if:

   a) the information contained therein remains accessible so as to be usable for a subsequent reference;

   b) the electronic record is retained in the format in which it was originally generated, sent or received or in a format which can be demonstrated to represent accurately the information originally generated, sent or received;

   c) the details which will facilitate the identification of the origin, destination, date and time of despatch or receipt of such electronic record are available in the electronic record:

   Provided that this clause does not apply to any information which is automatically generated solely for the purpose of enabling an electronic record to be despatched or received.

2) Nothing in this section shall apply to any law that expressly provides for the retention of documents,

records or information in the form of electronic records.

8. Publication of rule, regulation, etc., in Electronic Gazette

Where any law provides that any rule, regulation, order, bye-law, notification or any other matter shall be published in the *Official Gazette*, then, such requirement shall be deemed to have been satisfied if such rule, regulation, order, bye-law, notification or any other matter is published in the *Official Gazette* or *Electronic Gazette:*

Provided that where any rule, regulation, order, bye-law, notification or any other matter is published in the *Official Gazette* or *Electronic Gazette*, the date of publication shall be deemed to be the date of the *Gazette* which was first published in any form.

9. Sections 6,7 and 8 not to confer right to insist document should be accepted in electronic form

Nothing contained in sections 6, 7 and 8 shall confer a right upon any person to insist that any Ministry or Department of the Central Government or the State Government or any authority or body established by or under any law or controlled or funded by the Central or State Government should accept, issue, create, retain and preserve any document in the form of electronic records or effect any monetary transaction in the electronic form.

10. Power to make rules by Central Government in respect of digital signature

The Central Government may, for the purposes of this Act, by rules, prescribe:

a) the type of digital signature;

b) the manner and format in which the digital signature shall be affixed;

c) the manner or procedure which facilitates identification of the person affixing the digital signature;

d) control processes and procedures to ensure adequate integrity, security and confidentiality of electronic records or payments; and

e) any other matter which is necessary to give legal effect to digital signatures.

CHAPTER IV

ATTRIBUTION ACKNOWLEDGEMENT AND DESPATCH OF ELECTRONIC RECORDS

1. *Attribution of electronic records*

An electronic record shall be attributed to the originator:

a) if it was sent by the originator himself;

b) by a person who had the authority to act on behalf of the originator in respect of that electronic record; or

c) by an information system programmed by or on behalf of the originator to operate automatically.

12. *Acknowledgement of receipt*

1) Where the originator has not agreed with the addressee that the acknowledgment of receipt of electronic record be given in a particular form or by a particular method, an acknowledgment may be given by:

   a) any communication by the addressee, automated or otherwise; or

   b) any conduct of the addressee, sufficient to indicate to the originator that the electronic record has been received.

2) Where the originator has stipulated that the electronic record shall be binding only on receipt of an acknowledgment of such electronic record by him, then unless acknowledgement has been so received, the electronic record shall be deemed to have been never sent by the originator.

3) Where the originator has not stipulated that the electronic record shall be binding only on receipt of such acknowledgement, and the acknowledgement has not been received by the originator within the time specified or agreed or, if no time has been specified or agreed to within a reasonable time, then the originator may give notice to the addressee stating that no acknowledgement has been received by him and specifying a reasonable time by which the acknowledgement must be received by him and if no acknowledgement is received within the aforesaid time limit he may after giving notice to the addressee, treat the electronic record as though it has never been sent.

13. Time and place of despatch and receipt of electronic record

1) Save as otherwise agreed to between the originator and the addressee, the dispatch of an electronic record occurs when it enters a computer resource outside the control of the originator.

2) Save as otherwise agreed between the originator and the addressee, the time of receipt of an electronic record shall be determined as follows, namely:

   a) if the addressee has designated a computer resource for the purpose of receiving electronic records:

i) receipt occurs at the time when the electronic, record enters the designated computer resource; or

ii) if the electronic record is sent to a computer resource of the addressee that is not the designated computer resource, receipt occurs at the time when the electronic record is retrieved by the addressee;

b) if the addressee has not designated a computer resource along with specified timings, if any, receipt occurs when the electronic record enters the computer resource of the addressee.

3) Save as otherwise agreed to between the originator and the addressee, an electronic record is deemed to be dispatched at the place where the originator has his place of business, and is deemed to be received at the place where the addressee has his place of business.

4) The provisions of sub-section (2) shall apply notwithstanding that the place where the computer resource is located may be different from the place where the electronic record is deemed to have been received under sub-section (3).

5) For the purposes of this section:

a) if the originator or the addressee has more than one place of business, the principal place of business, shall be the place of business;

b) if the originator or the addressee does not have a place of business, his usual place of residence shall be deemed to be the place of business;

c) "usual place of residence", in relation to a body corporate, means the place where it is registered.

CHAPTER V

SECURE ELECTRONIC RECORD AND SECURE DIGITAL SIGNATURES

14. Secure electronic record

Where any security procedure has been applied to an electronic record at a specific point of time, then such record shall be deemed to be a secure electronic record from such point of time to the time of verification.

15. Secure digital signature

If, by application of a security procedure agreed to by the parties concerned, it can be verified that a digital signature, at the time it was affixed, was:

a) unique to the subscriber affixing it;

b) capable of identifying such subscriber;

c) created in a manner or using a means under the exclusive control of the subscriber and is linked to the electronic record to which it relates in such a manner that if the electronic record was altered the digital signature would be invalidated, then such digital signature shall be deemed to be a secure digital signature.

16. Security procedure

The Central Government shall for the purposes of this Act prescribe the security procedure having regard to commercial circumstances prevailing at the time when the procedure was used, including:

a) the nature of the transaction;

b) the level of sophistication of the parties with reference to their technological capacity;

c) the volume of similar transactions engaged in by other parties;

d) the availability of alternatives offered to but rejected by any party;

e) the cost of alternative procedures; and

f) the procedures in general use for similar types of transactions or communications.

CHAPTER VI

REGULATION OF CERTIFYING AUTHORITIES

17. Appointment of controller and other officers

1) The Central Government may, by notification in the Official Gazette, appoint a Controller of Certifying Authorities for the purposes of this Act and may also by the same or subsequent notification appoint such number of Deputy Controllers and Assistant Controllers as it deems fit.

2) The Controller shall discharge his functions under this Act subject to the general control and directions of the Central Government.

3) The Deputy Controllers and Assistant Controllers shall perform the functions assigned to them by the Controller under the general superintendence and control of the Controller.

4) The qualifications, experience and terms and conditions of service of Controller, Deputy Controllers and Assistant Controllers shall be such as may be prescribed by the Central Government.

5) The Head Office and Branch Office of the office of the Controller shall be at such places as the Central

Government may specify, and these may be established at such places as the Central Government may think fit.

6) There shall be a seal of the Office of the Controller.

18. Functions of controller

The Controller may perform all or any of the following functions, namely:

a) exercising supervision over the activities of the Certifying Authorities;

b) certifying public keys of the Certifying Authorities;

c) laying down the standards to be maintained by the Certifying Authorities;

d) specifying the qualifications and experience which employees of the Certifying Authorities should possess;

e) specifying the conditions subject to which the Certifying Authorities shall conduct their business;

f) specifying the contents of written, printed or visual materials and advertisements that may be distributed or used in respect of a Digital Signature Certificate and the public key;

g) specifying the form and content of a Digital Signature Certificate and the key,

h) specifying the form and manner in which accounts shall be maintained by the Certifying Authorities;

i) specifying the terms and conditions subject to which auditors may be appointed and the remuneration to be paid to them;

j) facilitating the establishment of any electronic system by a Certifying Authority either solely or jointly with other Certifying Authorities and regulation of such systems;

k) specifying the manner in which the Certifying Authorities shall conduct their dealings with the subscribers;

l) resolving any conflict of interests between the Certifying Authorities and the subscribers;

m) laying down the duties of the Certifying Authorities;

n) maintaining a data base containing the disclosure record of every Certifying Authority containing such particulars as may be specified by regulations, which shall be accessible to public.

19. Recognition of foreign certifying authorities

1) Subject to such conditions and restrictions as may be specified by regulations, the Controller may with the previous approval of the Central Government, and by notification in the Official Gazette, recognise any foreign Certifying Authority as a Certifying Authority for the purposes of this Act.

2) Where any Certifying Authority is recognised under sub-section (1), the Digital Signature Certificate issued by such Certifying Authority shall be valid for the purposes of this Act.

3) The Controller may, if he is satisfied that any Certifying Authority has contravened any of the conditions and restrictions subject to which it was granted recognition under sub-section (1) he may, for reasons to be recorded in writing, by notification in the Official Gazette, revoke such recognition.

20. Controller to act as repository

1) The Controller shall be the repository of all Digital Signature Certificates issued under this Act.

2) The Controller shall:

a) make use of hardware, software and procedures that are secure from intrusion and misuse;

b) observe such other standards as may be prescribed by the Central Government, to ensure that the secrecy and security of the digital signatures are assured.

3) The Controller shall maintain a computerised database of all public keys in such a manner that such database and the public keys are available to any member of the public.

21. Licence to issue digital signature certificates

1) Subject to the provisions of sub-section (2), any person may make an application, to the Controller, for a licence to issue Digital Signature Certificates.

2) No licence shall be issued under sub-section (1), unless the applicant fulfils such requirements with respect to qualification, expertise, manpower, financial resources and other infrastructure facilities, which are necessary to issue Digital Signature Certificates as may be prescribed by the Central Government.

3) A licence granted under this section shall:

a) be valid for such period as may be prescribed by the Central Government;

b) not be transferable or heritable;

c) be subject to such terms and conditions as may be specified by the regulations.

22. Application for licence

1) Every application for issue of a licence shall be in such form as may be prescribed by the Central Government.

2) Every application for issue of a licence shall be accompanied by:

   a) a certification practice statement;

   b) a statement including the procedures with respect to identification of the applicant;

   c) payment of such fees, not exceeding twenty-five thousand rupees as may be prescribed by the Central Government;

   d) such other documents, as may be prescribed by the Central Government.

23. Renewal of licence

An application for renewal of a licence shall be:

a) in such form;

b) accompanied by such fees, not exceeding five thousand rupees, as may be prescribed by the Central Government and shall be made not less than forty-five days before the date of expiry of the period of validity of the licence.

24. Procedure for grant or rejection of licence

The Controller may, on receipt of an application under sub-section (1) of section 21, after considering the documents accompanying the application and such other factors, as he deems fit, grant the licence or reject the application:

Provided that no application shall be rejected under this section unless the applicant has been given a reasonable opportunity of presenting his case.

25. Suspension of licence

1) The Controller may, if he is satisfied after making such inquiry, as he may think fit, that a Certifying Authority has:

a) made a statement in, or in relation to, the application for the issue or renewal of the licence, which is incorrect or false in material particulars;

b) failed to comply with the terms and conditions subject to which the licence was granted;

c) failed to maintain the standards specified under clause (b) of sub-section (2) of section 20;

d) contravened any provisions of this Act, rule, regulation or order made thereunder,

Revoke the licence

Provided that no licence shall be revoked unless the Certifying Authority has been given a reasonable opportunity of showing cause against the proposed revocation.

2) The Controller may, if he has reasonable cause to believe that there is any ground for revoking a licence under sub-section (1), by order suspend such licence pending the completion of any inquiry ordered by him:

Provided that no licence shall be suspended for a period exceeding ten days unless the Certifying Authority has been given a reasonable opportunity of showing cause against the proposed suspension.

3) No Certifying Authority whose licence has been suspended shall issue any Digital Signature Certificate during such suspension.

26. Notice of suspension or revocation of licence

1) Where the licence of the Certifying Authority is suspended or revoked, the Controller shall publish notice of such suspension or revocation, as the case may be, in the database maintained by him.

2) Where one or more repositories are specified, the Controller shall publish notices of such suspension or revocation, as the case may be, in all such repositories:

   Provided that the database containing the notice of such suspension or revocation, as the case may be, shall be made available through a website which shall be accessible round the clock:

   Provided further that the Controller may, if he considers necessary, publicise the contents of database in such electronic or other media, as he may consider appropriate.

27. Power to delegate

The Controller may, in writing, authorise the Deputy Controller, Assistant Controller or any officer to exercise any of the powers of the Controller under this Chapter.

28. Power to investigate contraventions

1) The Controller or any officer authorised by him in this behalf shall take up for investigation any contravention of the provisions of this Act, rules or regulations made thereunder.

2) The Controller or any officer authorised by him in this behalf shall exercise the like powers which are conferred on Income-tax authorities under Chapter XIII of the Income-tax Act, 1961 and shall exercise such powers, subject to such limitations laid down under that Act.

29. Access to computers and data

1) Without prejudice to the provisions of sub-section (1) of section 69, the Controller or any person authorised by him shall, if he has reasonable cause to suspect that any contravention of the provisions of this Act, rules or regulations made thereunder has been

committed, have access to any computer system, any apparatus, data or any other material connected with such system, for the purpose of searching or causing a search to be made for obtaining any information or data contained in or available to such computer system.

2) For the purposes of sub-section (1), the Controller or any person authorised by him may, by order, direct any person in charge of, or otherwise concerned with the operation of, the computer system, data apparatus or material, to provide him with such reasonable technical and other assistance as he may consider necessary.

30. Certifying authority to follow certain procedures

Every Certifying Authority shall:

a) make use of hardware, software and procedures that are secure from intrusion and misuse;

b) provide a reasonable level of reliability in its services which are reasonably suited to the performance of intended functions;

c) adhere to security procedures to ensure that the secrecy and privacy of the digital signatures are assured; and

d) observe such other standards as may be specified by regulations.

31. Certifying authority to ensure compliance of the Act, etc.

Every Certifying Authority shall ensure that every person employed or otherwise engaged by it complies, in the course of his employment or engagement, with the provisions of this Act, rules, regulations and orders made thereunder.

32. Display of licence

Every Certifying Authority shall display its licence at a conspicuous place of the premises in which it carries on its business.

33. Surrender of licence

1) Every Certifying Authority whose licence is suspended or revoked shall immediately after such suspension or revocation, surrender the licence to the Controller.
2) Where any Certifying Authority fails to surrender a licence under sub-section (1), the person in whose favour a licence is issued, shall be guilty of an offence and shall be punished with imprisonment which may extend up to six months or a fine which may extend up to ten thousand rupees or with both.

34. Disclosure

1) Every Certifying Authority shall disclose in the manner specified by regulations:
    a) its Digital Signature Certificate which contains the public key corresponding to the private key used by that Certifying Authority to digitally sign another Digital Signature Certificate;
    b) any certification practice statement relevant thereto;
    c) notice of the revocation or suspension of its Certifying Authority certificate, if any; and
    d) any other fact that materially and adversely affects either the reliability of a Digital Signature Certificate, which that Authority has issued, or the Authority's ability to perform its services.
2) Wherein the opinion of the Certifying Authority any event has occurred or any situation has arisen which

may materially and adversely affect the integrity of its computer system or the conditions subject to which a Digital Signature Certificate was granted, then, the Certifying Authority shall:

a) use reasonable efforts to notify any person who is likely to be affected by that occurrence; or

b) act in accordance with the procedure specified in its certification practice statement to deal with such event or situation.

CHAPTER VII

DIGITAL SIGNATURE CERTIFICATES

35. Certifying authority to issue digital signature certificate

1) Any person may make an application to the Certifying Authority for the issue of a Digital Signature Certificate in such form as may be prescribed by the Central Govern-ment.

2) Every such application shall be accompanied by such fee not exceeding twenty-five thousand rupees as may be prescribed by the Central Government, to be paid to the Certifying Authority:

   Provided that while prescribing fees under sub-section (2) different fees may be prescribed for different classes of applicants.

3) Every such application shall be accompanied by a certification practice statement or where there is no such statement, a statement containing such particulars, as may be specified by regulations.

4) On receipt of an application under sub-section (1), the Certifying Authority may, after consideration of the certification practice statement or the other statement under sub-section (3) and after making such enquiries

as it may deem fit, grant the Digital Signature Certificate or for reasons to be recorded in writing, reject the application:

Provided that no Digital Signature Certificate shall be granted unless the Certifying Authority is satisfied that:

a) the applicant holds the private key corresponding to the public key to be listed in the Digital Signature Certificate;

b) the applicant holds a private key, which is capable of creating a digital signature;

c) the public key to be listed in the certificate can be used to verify a digital signature affixed by the private key held by the applicant:

Provided further that no application shall be rejected unless the applicant has been given a reasonable opportunity of showing cause against the proposed rejection.

36. Representations upon issuance of digital signature certificate

A Certifying Authority while issuing a Digital Signature Certificate shall certify that:

a) it has complied with the provisions of this Act and the rules and regulations made thereunder,

b) it has published the Digital Signature Certificate or otherwise made it available to such person relying on it and the subscriber has accepted it;

c) the subscriber holds the private key corresponding to the public key, listed in the Digital Signature Certificate;

d) the subscriber's public key and private key constitute a functioning key pair,

e) the information contained in the Digital Signature Certificate is accurate; and

f) it has no knowledge of any material fact, which if it had been included in the Digital Signature Certificate would adversely affect the reliability of the representations made in clauses (a) to (d).

37. Suspension of digital signature certificate

1) Subject to the provisions of sub-section (2), the Certifying Authority which has issued a Digital Signature Certificate may suspend such Digital Signature Certificate:

    a) on receipt of a request to that effect from:

        i) the subscriber listed in toe Digital Signature Certificate; or

        ii) any person duly authorised to act on behalf of that subscriber.

    b) if it is of opinion that the Digital Signature Certificate should be suspended in public interest.

2) A Digital Signature Certificate shall not be suspended for a period exceeding fifteen days unless the subscriber has been given an opportunity of being heard in the matter.

3) On suspension of a Digital Signature Certificate under this section, the Certifying Authority shall communicate the same to the subscriber.

38. Revocation of digital signature certificate

1) A Certifying Authority may revoke a Digital Signature Certificate issued by it:

a) where the subscriber or any other person authorised by him makes a request to that effect; or

b) upon the death of the subscriber, or

c) upon the dissolution of the firm or winding up of the company where the subscriber is a firm or a company.

2) Subject to the provisions of sub-section (3) and without prejudice to the provisions of sub-section (1), a Certifying Authority may revoke a Digital Signature Certificate which has been issued by it at any time, if it is of opinion that:

a) a material fact represented in the Digital Signature Certificate is false or has been concealed;

b) a requirement for issuance of the Digital Signature Certificate was not satisfied;

c) the Certifying Authority's private key or security system was compromised in a manner materially affecting the Digital Signature Certificate's reliability;

d) the subscriber has been declared insolvent or dead or where a subscriber is a firm or a company, which has been dissolved, wound-up or otherwise ceased to exist.

3) A Digital Signature Certificate shall not be revoked unless the subscriber has been given an opportunity of being heard in the matter.

4) On revocation of a Digital Signature Certificate under this section, the Certifying Authority shall communicate the same to the subscriber.

39. Notice of suspension or revocation

1) Where a Digital Signature Certificate is suspended or

revoked under section 37 or section 38, the Certifying Authority shall publish a notice of such suspension or revocation, as the case may be, in the repository specified in the Digital Signature Certificate for publication of such notice.

2) Where one or more repositories are specified, the Certifying Authority shall publish notices of such suspension or revocation, as the case may be in all such repositories.

CHAPTER VIII

DUTIES OF SUBSCRIBERS

40. Generating key pair

Where any Digital Signature Certificate, the public key of which corresponds to the private key of that subscriber which is to be listed in the Digital Signature Certificate has been accepted by a subscriber, then, the subscriber shall generate the key pair by applying the security procedure.

41. Acceptance of digital signature certificate

1) A subscriber shall be deemed to have accepted a Digital Signature Certificate if he publishes or authorises the publication of a Digital Signature Certificate:

   a) to one or more persons;

   b) in a repository, or otherwise demonstrates his approval of the Digital Signature Certificate in any manner.

2) By accepting a Digital Signature Certificate the subscriber certifies to all who reasonably rely on the information contained in the Digital Signature Certificate that:

a) the subscriber holds the private key corresponding to the public key listed in the Digital Signature Certificate and is entitled to hold the same;

b) all representations made by the subscriber to the Certifying Authority and all material relevant to the information contained in the Digital Signature Certificate are true;

c) all information in the Digital Signature Certificate that is within the knowledge of the subscriber is true.

42. Control of private key

1) Every subscriber shall exercise reasonable care to retain control of the private key corresponding to the public key listed in his Digital Signature Certificate and take all steps to prevent its disclosure to a person not authorised to affix the digital signature of the subscriber.

2) If the private key corresponding to the public key listed in the Digital Signature Certificate has been compromised, then, the subscriber shall communicate the same without any delay to the Certifying Authority in such manner as may be specified by the regulations.

   Explanation: For the removal of doubts, it is hereby declared that the subscriber shall be liable till he has informed the Certifying Authority that the private key has been compromised.

CHAPTER IX

PENALTIES AND ADJUDICATION

43. Penalty for damage to computer, computer system, etc.

If any person without permission of the owner or any

other person who is incharge of a computer, computer system or computer network:

a) accesses or secures access to such computer, computer system or computer network;
b) downloads, copies or extracts any data, computer database or information from such computer, computer system or computer network including information or data held or stored in any removable storage medium;
c) introduces or causes to be introduced any computer contaminant or computer virus into any computer, computer system or computer network;
d) damages or causes to be damaged any computer, computer system or computer network, data, computer database or any other programmes residing in such computer, computer system or computer network;
e) disrupts or causes disruption of any computer, computer system or computer network;
f) denies or causes the denial of access to any person authorised to access any computer, computer system or computer network by any means;
g) provides any assistance to any person to facilitate access to a computer, computer system or computer network in contravention of the provisions of this Act, rules or regulations made thereunder;
h) charges the services availed of by a person to the account of another person by tampering with or manipulating any computer, computer system, or computer network, he shall be liable to pay damages by way of compensation not exceeding one crore rupees to the person so affected.

   Explanation: For the purposes of this section:

   i) "computer contaminant" means any set of computer instructions that are designed:

a) to modify, destroy, record, transmit data or pro-gramme residing within a computer, computer system or computer network; or

b) by any means to usurp the normal operation of the computer, computer system, or computer network;

ii) "computer database" means a representation of information, knowledge, facts, concepts or instructions in text, image, audio, video that are being prepared or have been prepared in a formalised manner or have been produced by a computer, computer system or computer network and are intended for use in a computer, computer system or computer network;

iii) "computer virus" means any computer instruction, information, data or programme that destroys, damages, degrades or adversely affects the performance of a computer resource or attaches itself to another computer resource and operates when a programme, daia or instruction is executed or some other event takes place in that computer resource;

iv) "damage" means to destroy, alter, delete, add, modify or rearrange any computer resource by any means.

44. Penalty for failure to furnish information return, etc.

If any person who is required under this Act or any rules or regulations made thereunder to:

a) furnish any document, return or report to the Controller or the Certifying Authority fails to furnish the same, he shall be liable to a penalty not exceeding one lakh and fifty thousand rupees for each such failure;

b) file any return or furnish any information, books or other documents within the time specified therefor in the regulations fails to file return or furnish the same within the time specified therefore in the regulations, he shall be liable to a penalty not exceeding five thousand rupees for every day during which such failure continues;

c) maintain books of account or records, fails to maintain the same, he shall be liable to a penalty not exceeding ten thousand rupees for every day during which the failure continues.

45. Residuary penalty

Whoever contravenes any rules or regulations made under this Act, for the contravention of which no penalty has been separately provided, shall be liable to pay a compensation not exceeding twenty-five thousand rupees to the person affected by such contravention or a penalty not exceeding twenty-five thousand rupees.

46. Power to adjudicate

1) For the purpose of adjudging under this Chapter whether any person has committed a contravention of any of the provisions of this Act or of any rule, regulation, direction or order made thereunder the Central Government shall, subject to the provisions of sub-section (3), appoint any officer not below the rank of a Director to the Government of India or an equivalent officer of a State Government to be an adjudicating officer for holding an inquiry in the manner prescribed by the Central Government.

2) The adjudicating officer shall, after giving the person referred to in sub-section (1) a reasonable opportunity for making representation in the matter and if, on such inquiry, he is satisfied that the person has committed

the contravention, he may impose such penalty or award such compensation as he thinks fit in accordance with the provisions of that section.

3) No person shall be appointed as an adjudicating officer unless he possesses such experience in the field of Information Technology and legal or judicial experience as may be prescribed by the Central Government.

4) Where more than one adjudicating officers are appointed, the Central Government shall specify by order the matters and places with respect to which such officers shall exercise their jurisdiction.

5) Every adjudicating officer shall have the powers of a civil court which are conferred oh the Cyber Appellate Tribunal under sub-section (2) of section 58, and:

   a) all proceedings before it shall be deemed to be judicial proceedings within the meaning of sections 193 and 228 of the Indian Penal Code;

   b) shall be deemed to be a civil court for the purposes of sections 345 and 346 of the Code of Criminal Procedure, 1973.

47. Factors to be taken into account by the adjudicating officer

While adjudging the quantum of compensation under this Chapter, the adjudicating officer shall have due regard to the following factors, namely:

a) the amount of gain of unfair advantage, wherever quantifiable, made as a result of the default;

b) the amount of loss caused to any person as a result of the default;

c) the repetitive nature of the default.

CHAPTER X

THE CYBER REGULATIONS APPELLATE TRIBUNAL

48. Establishment of cyber appellate tribunal

1) The Central Government shall, by notification, establish one or more appellate tribunals to be known as the Cyber Regulations Appellate Tribunal.

2) The Central Government shall also specify, in the notification referred to in sub-section (1), the matters and places in relation to which the Cyber Appellate Tribunal may exercise jurisdiction.

49. Composition of cyber appellate tribunal

A Cyber Appellate Tribunal shall consist of one person only (hereinafter referred to as the Residing Officer of the Cyber Appellate Tribunal) to be appointed, by notification, by the Central Government.

50. Qualifications for appointment as presiding officer of the Cyber Appellate Tribunal

A person shall not be qualified for appointment as the Presiding Officer of a Cyber Appellate Tribunal unless he:

a) is, or has been or is qualified to be, a Judge of a High Court; or

b) is or has been a member of the Indian Legal Service and is holding or has held a post in Grade I of that Service for at least three years.

51. Term of office

The Presiding Officer of a Cyber Appellate Tribunal shall hold office for a term of five years from the date on which he enters upon his office or until he attains the age of sixty-five years, whichever is earlier.

52. Salary, allowances and other terms and conditions of service of presiding officer

The salary and allowances payable to, and the other terms and conditions of service including pension, gratuity and other retirement benefits of the Presiding Officer of a Cyber Appellate Tribunal shall be such as may be prescribed:

Provided that neither the salary and allowances nor the other terms and conditions of service of the Presiding Officer shall be varied to his disadvantage after appointment.

53. Filling up of vacancies

If, for reason other than temporary absence, any vacancy occurs in the office of the Presiding Officer of a Cyber Appellate Tribunal, then the Central Government shall appoint another person in accordance with the provisions of this Act to fill the vacancy and the proceedings may be continued before the Cyber Appellate Tribunal from the stage at which the vacancy is filled.

54. Resignation and removal

1) The Presiding Officer of a Cyber Appellate Tribunal may, by notice in writing under his hand addressed to the Central Government, resign his office:

   Provided that the said Presiding Officer shall, unless he is permitted by the Central Government to relinquish his office sooner, continue to hold office until the expiry of three months from the date of receipt of such notice or until a person duly appointed as his successor enters upon his office or until the expiry of his term of office, whichever is the earliest.

2) The Presiding Officer of a Cyber Appellate Tribunal shall not be removed from his office except by an order by the Central Government on the ground of

proved misbehaviour or incapacity after an inquiry made by a Judge of the Supreme Court in which the Presiding Officer concerned has been informed of the charges against him and given a reasonable opportunity of being heard in respect of these charges.

3) The Central Government may, by rules, regulate the procedure for the investigation of misbehaviour or incapacity of the aforesaid Presiding Officer.

55. Orders constituting Appellate Tribunal to be final and not to invalidate its proceedings

No order of the Central Government appointing any person as the Presiding Officer of a Cyber Appellate Tribunal shall be called in question in any manner and no act or proceeding before a Cyber Appellate Tribunal shall be called in question in any manner on the ground merely of any defect in the constitution of a Cyber Appellate Tribunal.

56. Staff of the cyber appellate tribunal

1) The Central Government shall provide the Cyber Appellate Tribunal with such officers and employees as that Government may think fit.
2) The officers and employees of the Cyber Appellate Tribunal shall discharge their functions under general superintendence of the Presiding Officer.
3) The salaries, allowances and other conditions of service of the officers and employees or the Cyber Appellate Tribunal shall be such as may be prescribed by the Central Government.

57. Appeal to cyber appellate tribunal

1) Save as provided in sub-section (2), any person aggrieved by an order made by Controller or an

adjudicating officer under this Act may prefer an appeal to a Cyber Appellate Tribunal having jurisdiction in the matter.

2) No appeal shall lie to the Cyber Appellate Tribunal from an order made by an adjudicating officer with the consent of the parties.

3) Every appeal under sub-section (1) shall be filed within a period of twenty-five days from the date on which a copy of the order made by the Controller or the adjudicating officer is received by the person aggrieved and it shall be in such form and be accompanied by such fee as may be prescribed:

   Provided that the Cyber Appellate Tribunal may entertain an appeal after the expiry of the said period of twenty-five days if it is satisfied that there was sufficient cause tor not filing it within that period.

4) On receipt of an appeal under sub-section (1), the Cyber Appellate Tribunal may, after giving the parties to the appeal, an opportunity of being heard, pass such orders thereon as it thinks fit, confirming, modifying or setting aside the order appealed against.

5) The Cyber Appellate Tribunal shall send a copy of every order made by it to the parties to the appeal and to the concerned Controller or adjudicating officer.

6) The appeal filed before the Cyber Appellate Tribunal under sub-section (1) shall be dealt with by it as expeditiously as possible and endeavour shall be made by it to dispose of the appeal finally within six months from the date of receipt of the appeal.

58. Procedure and powers of the cyber appellate tribunal

1) The Cyber Appellate Tribunal shall not be bound by the procedure laid down by the Code of civil

Procedure, 1908 but shall be guided by the principles of natural justice and, subject to the other provisions of this Act and of any rules, the Cyber Appellate Tribunal shall have powers to regulate its own procedure including the place at which it shall have its sittings.

2) The Cyber Appellate Tribunal shall have, for the purposes of discharging its functions under this Act, the same powers as are vested in a civil court under the Code of Civil Procedure, 1908, while trying a suit, in respect of the following matters, namely:

   a) summoning and enforcing the attendance of any person and examining him on oath;

   b) requiring the discovery and production of documents or other electronic records;

   c) receiving evidence on affidavits;

   d) issuing commissions for the examination of witnesses or documents;

   e) reviewing its decisions;

   f) dismissing an application for default or deciding it *ex pane;*

   g) any other matter which may be prescribed.

3) Every proceeding before the Cyber Appellate Tribunal shall be deemed to be a judicial proceeding within the meaning of sections 193 and 228, and for the purposes of section 196 of the Indian Penal Code and the Cyber Appellate Tribunal shall be deemed to be a civil court for the purposes of section 195 and Chapter XXVI of the Code of Criminal Procedure, 1973.

59. Right to legal representation

The appellant may either appear in person or authorise one or more legal practitioners or any of its officers to present his or its case before the Cyber Appellate Tribunal.

60. Limitation

The provisions of the Limitation Act, 1963, shall, as far as may be, apply to an appeal made to the Cyber Appellate Tribunal.

61. Civil court not to have jurisdiction

No court shall have jurisdiction to entertain any suit or proceeding in respect of any matter which an adjudicating officer appointed under this Act or the Cyber Appellate Tribunal constituted under this Act is empowered by or under this Act to determine and no injunction shall be granted by any court or other authority in respect of any action taken or to be taken in pursuance of any power conferred by or under this Act.

62. Appeal to high court

Any person aggrieved by any decision or order of the Cyber Appellate Tribunal may file an appeal to the High Court within sixty days from the date of communication of the decision or order of the Cyber Appellate Tribunal to him on any question of fact or law arising out of such order.

Provided that the High Court may, if it is satisfied that the appellant was prevented by sufficient cause from filing the appeal within the said period, allow it to be filed within a further period not exceeding sixty days.

63. Compounding of contraventions

1) Any contravention under this Chapter may, either before or after the institution of adjudication proceedings, be compounded by the Controller or such other officer as may be specially authorised by him in this behalf or by the adjudicating officer, as the case

may be, subject to such conditions as the Controller or such other officer or the adjudicating officer may specify:

Provided that such sum shall not, in any case, exceed the maximum amount of the penalty which may be imposed under this Act for the contravention so compounded.

2) Nothing in sub-section (1) shall apply to a person who commits the same or similar contravention within a period of three years from the date on which the first contravention, committed by him, was compounded.

Explanation: For the purposes of this sub-section, any second or subsequent contravention committed after the expiry of a period of three years from the date on which the contravention was previously compounded shall be deemed to be a first contravention.

3) Where any contravention has been compounded under sub-section (1), no proceeding or further proceeding, as the case may be, shall be taken against the person guilty of such contravention in respect of the contravention so compounded.

64. Recovery of penalty

A penalty imposed under this Act, if it is not paid, shall be recovered as an area of land revenue and the licence or the Digital Signature Certificate, as the case may be, shall be suspended till the penalty is paid.

CHAPTER XI

OFFENCES

65. Tampering with computer source documents

Whoever knowingly or intentionally conceals, destroys or alters or intentionally or knowingly causes another to conceal, destroy or alter any computer source code used for a computer, computer programme, computer system or computer network, when the computer source code is required to be kept or maintained by law for the time being in force, shall be punishable with imprisonment up to three years, or with fine which may extend up to two lakh rupees, or with both.

Explanation.—For the purposes of this section, 'computer source code' means the listing of programmes, computer commands, design and layout and programme analysis of computer resource in any form.

66. Hacking with computer system

1) Whoever with the intent to cause or knowing that he is likely to cause wrongful loss or damage to the public or any person destroys or deletes or alters any information residing in a computer resource or diminishes its value or utility or affects it injuriously by any means, commits hack:

2) Whoever commits hacking shall be punished with imprisonment up to three years, or with fine which may extend upto two lakh rupees, or with both.

67. Publishing of information which is obscene in electronic form

Whoever publishes or transmits or causes to be published in the electronic form, any material which is lascivious or appeals to the prurient interest or if its effect is such as to tend to deprave and corrupt persons who are likely, having regard to all relevant circumstances, to read, see or hear the matter contained or embodied in it, shall be punished on first conviction with imprisonment of either description for a term which may extend to five years and with fine which may extend to one lakh rupees and in the event of a second or subsequent conviction with imprisonment of either description for a term which may extend to ten years and also with fine which may extend to two lakh rupees.

68. Power of Controller to give directions

1) The Controller may, by order, direct a Certifying Authority or any employee of such Authority to take such measures or cease carrying on such activities as specified in the order if those are necessary to ensure compliance with the provisions of this Act, rules or any regulations made thereunder.

2) Any person who fails to comply with any order under sub-section (1) shall be guilty of an offence and shall be liable on conviction to imprisonment for a term not exceeding three years or to a fine not exceeding two lakh rupees or to both.

69. Directions of Controller to a subscriber to extend facilities to decrypt information

1) If the Controller is satisfied that it is necessary or expedient so to do in the interest of the sovereignty or integrity of India, the security of the State, friendly relations with foreign Stales or public order or for preventing incitement to the commission of any cognizable offence, for reasons to be recorded in writing, by order, direct any agency of the Government to intercept any information transmitted through any computer resource.

2) The subscriber or any person incharge of the computer resource shall, when called upon by any agency which has been directed under sub-section (1), extend all facilities and technical assistance to decrypt the information.

3) The subscriber or any person who fails to assist the agency referred to in sub-section (2) shall be punished with an imprisonment for a term which may extend to seven years.

70. Protected system

1) The appropriate Government may, by notification in the *Official Gazette*, declare that any computer, computer system or computer network to be a protected system.

2) The appropriate Government may, by order in writing, authorise the persons who are authorised to access protected systems notified under sub-section (1).

3) Any person who secures access or attempts to secure access to a protected system in contravention of the provisions of this section shall be punished with imprisonment of either description for a term which may extend to ten years and shall also be liable to fine.

71. Penalty for misrepresentation

Whoever makes any misrepresentation to, or suppresses any material fact from, the Controller or the Certifying Authority for obtaining any licence or Digital Signature Certificate, as the case may be shall be punished with imprisonment for a term which may extend to two years, or with fine which may extend to one lakh rupees, or with both.

72. Penalty for breach of confidentiality and privacy

Save as otherwise provided in this Act or any other law for the time being in force, any person who, in pursuance of any of the powers conferred under this Act, rules or regulations made thereunder, has secured access to any electronic record, book, register, correspondence, information, document or other material without the consent of the person concerned discloses such electronic record, book, register, correspondence, information, document or other material to any other person shall be punished with imprisonment for a term which may extend to two years, or with fine which may extend to one lakh rupees, or with both.

73. Penalty for publishing Digital Signature Certificate false in certain particulars

1) No person shall publish a Digital Signature Certificate or otherwise make it available to any other person with the knowledge that:

    a) the Certifying Authority listed in the certificate has not issued it; or

    b) the subscriber listed in the certificate has not accepted it; or

    c) the certificate has been revoked or suspended, unless such publication is for the purpose of verifying a digital signature created prior to such suspension or revocation.

2) Any person who contravenes the provisions of sub-section (1) shall be punished with imprisonment for a term which may extend to two years, or with fine which may extend to one lakh rupees, or with both.

74. Publication for fraudulent purpose

Whoever knowingly creates, publishes or otherwise makes available a Digital Signature Certificate for any fraudulent or unlawful purpose shall be punished with imprisonment for a term which may extend to two years, or with fine which may extend to one lakh rupees, or with both.

75. Act to apply for offence or contravention committed outside India

1) Subject to the provisions of sub-section (2), the provisions of this Act shall apply also to any offence or contravention committed outside India by any person irrespective of his nationality.

2) For the purposes of sub-section (1), this Act shall apply to an offence or contravention committed outside India by any person if the act or conduct constituting the offence or contravention involves a computer, computer system or computer network located in India.

76. Confiscation

Any computer, computer system, floppies, compact disks, tape drives or any other accessories related thereto, in respect of which any provision of this Act, rules, orders or regulations made thereunder has been or is being contravened, shall be liable to confiscation:

Provided that where it is established to the satisfaction of the court adjudicating the confiscation that the person in whose possession, power or control of any such computer, computer system, floppies, compact disks, tape drives or any other accessories relating thereto is found is not responsible for the contravention of the provisions of this Act, rules, orders or regulations made thereunder, the court may, instead of making an order for confiscation of such computer, computer system, floppies, compact disks, tape drives or any other accessories related thereto, make such other order authorised by this Act against the person contravening of the provisions of this Act, rules, orders or regulations made thereunder as it may think fit.

77. Penalties or confiscation not to interfere with other punishments

No penalty imposed or confiscation made under this Act shall prevent the imposition of any other punishment to which the person affected thereby is liable under any other law for the time being in force.

78. Power to investigate offences

Notwithstanding anything contained in the Code of

Criminal Procedure, 1973, a police officer not below the rank of Deputy Superintendent of Police shall investigate any offence under this Act.

CHAPTER XII

NETWORK SERVICE PROVIDERS NOT TO BE LIABLE IN CERTAIN CASES

79. Network service providers not to be liable in certain cases

For the removal of doubts, it is hereby declared that no person providing any service as a network service provider shall be liable under this Act, rules or regulations made thereunder for any third party information or data made available by him if he proves that the offence or contravention was committed without his knowledge or that he had exercised all due diligence to prevent the commission of such offence or contravention.

Explanation: For the purposes of this section:

a) "network service provider" means an intermediary;

b) "third party information" means any information dealt with by a network service provider in his capacity as an intermediary.

CHAPTER XIIL

MISCELLANEOUS

80. Power of police officer and other officers to enter, search, etc.

1) Notwithstanding anything contained in the Code of Criminal Procedure, 1973, any police officer, not below

the rank of a Deputy Superintendent of Police, or any other officer of the Central Government or a State Government authorised by the Central Government in this behalf may enter any public place and search and arrest without warrant any person found therein who is reasonably suspected or having committed or of committing or of being about to commit any offence under this Act

Explanation: For the purposes of this sub-section, the expression "public place" includes any public conveyance, any hotel, any shop or any other place intended for use by, or accessible to the public.

2) Where any person is arrested under sub-section (1) by an officer other than a police officer, such officer shall, without unnecessary delay, take or send the person arrested before a magistrate having jurisdiction in the case or before the officer-in-charge of a police station.

3) The provisions of the Code of Criminal Procedure, 1973 shall, subject to the provisions of this section, apply, so far as may be, in relation to any entry, search or arrest, made under this section.

81. Act to have overriding effect

The provisions of this Act shall have effect notwithstanding anything inconsistent therewith contained in any other law for the time being in force.

82. Controller, deputy controller and assistant controllers to be public servants

The Presiding Officer and other officers and employees of a Cyber Appellate Tribunal, the Controller, the Deputy Controller and the Assistant Controllers shall be deemed to be public servants within the meaning of section 21 of the Indian Penal Code.

83. Power to give directions

The Central Government may give directions to any State Government as to the carrying into execution in the State of any of the provisions of this Act or of any rule, regulation or order made thereunder.

84. Protection of action taken in good faith

No suit, prosecution or other legal proceeding shall lie against the Central Government, the State Government, the Controller or any person acting on behalf of him, the Presiding Officer, adjudicating officers and the staff of the Cyber Appellate Tribunal for anything which is in good faith done or intended to be done in pursuance of this Act or any rule, regulation or order made thereunder.

85. Offences by companies

1) Where a person committing a contravention of any of the provisions of this Act or of any rule, direction or order made thereunder is a company, every person who, at the time the contravention was committed, was in charge of, and was responsible to, the company for the conduct of business of the company as well as the company, shall be guilty of the contravention and shall be liable to be proceeded against and punished accordingly:

   Provided that nothing contained in this sub-section shall render any such person liable to punishment if he proves that the contravention took place without his knowledge or that he exercised all due diligence to prevent such contravention.

2) Notwithstanding anything contained in sub-section (1), where a contravention of any of the provisions of this Act or of any rule, direction or order made thereunder has been committed by a company and it is proved that the contravention has taken place with the

consent or connivance of, or is attributable to any neglect on the part of, any director, manager, secretary or other officer of the company, such director, manager, secretary or other officer shall also be deemed to be guilty of the contravention and shall be liable to be proceeded against and punished accordingly.

Explanation: For the purposes of this section:

i) "company" means any body corporate and includes a firm or other association of individuals; and

ii) "director", in relation to a firm, means a partner in the firm.

86. Removal of difficulties

1) If any difficulty arises in giving effect to the provisions of this Act, the Central Government may, by order published in the *Official Gazette*, make such provisions not inconsistent with the provisions of this Act as appear to it to be necessary or expedient for removing the difficulty:

Provided that no order shall be made under this section after the expiry of a period of two years from the commencement of this Act.

2) Every order made under this section shall be laid, as soon as may be after it is made, before each House of Parliament.

87. Power of central government to make rules

1) The Central Government may, by notification in the *Official Gazette* and in the *Electronic Gazette* make rules to carry out the provisions of this Act

2) In particular, and without prejudice to the generality of the foregoing power, such rules may provide for all or any of the following mailers, namely:

   a) the manner in which any information or matter may be authenticated by means of digital signature under section 5;

   b) the electronic form in which filing, issue, grant or payment shall be effected under sub-section (1) of section 6;

   c) the manner and format in which electronic records shall be filed, or issued and the method of .payment under sub-section (2) of section 6;

   d) the matters relating to the type of digital signature, manner and format in which it may be affixed under section 10;

   e) the security procedure for the purpose of creating secure electronic record and secure digital signature under section 16;

   f) the qualifications, experience and terms and conditions of service of Controller, Deputy Controllers and Assistant Controllers under section 17;

   g) other standards to be observed by the Controller under clause (b) of subsection (2) of section 20;

   h) the requirements which an applicant must fulfil under sub-section (2) of section 21;

   i) the period of validity of licence granted under clause (a) of sub-section (3) of section 21;

   j) the form in which an application for licence may be made under sub-section (1) of section 22;

k) the amount of fees payable under clause (c) of sub-section (2) of section 22;

l) such other documents which shall accompany an application for licence under clause (a) of sub-section (2) of section 22;

m) the form and the fee for renewal of a licence and the fee payable there of under section 23;

n) the form in which application for issue of a Digital Signature Certificate may be made under sub-section (1) of section 35;

o) the fee to be paid to the Certifying Authority for issue of a Digital Signature Certificate under sub-section (2) of section 35;

p) the manner in which the adjudicating officer shall hold inquiry under subsection (1) of section 46;

q) the qualification and experience which the adjudicating officer shall possess under sub-section (3) of section 46;

r) the salary, allowances and the other terms and conditions of service of the Presiding Officer under section 52;

s) the procedure for invėstigation of misbehaviour or incapacity of the Presiding Officer under sub-section (3) of section 54;

t) the salary and allowances and other conditions of service of other officers and employees under sub-section (3} of section 56;

u) the form in which appeal may be filed and the fee thereof under sub -section (3) of section 57;

v) any other power of a civil court required to be prescribed under clause (g) of sub-section (2) of section 58; and

w) any other matter which is required to be, or may be, prescribed.

3) Every notification made by the Central Government under clause (f) of subsection (4) of section 1 and every rule made by it shall be laid, as soon as may be after it is made, before each House of Parliament, while it is in session, for a total period of thirty days which may be comprised in one session or in two or more successive sessions, and if, before the expiry of the session immediately following the session or the successive sessions aforesaid, both Houses agree in making any modification in the notification or the rule or both Houses agree that the notification or the rule should not be made, the notification or the rule shall thereafter have effect only in such modified form or be of no effect, as the case may be; so, however, that any such modification or annulment shall be without prejudice to the validity of anything previously done under that notification or rule.

88. Constitution of advisory committee

1) The Central Government shall, as soon as may be after the commencement of this Act, constitute a Committee called the Cyber Regulations Advisory Committee.

2) The Cyber Regulations Advisory Committee shall consist of a Chairperson and such number of other official and non-official members representing the interests principally affected or having special knowledge of the subject-matter as the Central Government may deem fit.

3) The Cyber Regulations Advisory Committee shall advise:

   a) the Central Government either generally as regards any rules or for any other purpose connected with this Act;

b) the Controller in framing the regulations under this Act.

4) There shall be paid to the non-official members of such Committee such travelling and other allowances as the Central Government may fix.

89. Power of controller to make regulations

1) The Controller may, after consultation with the Cyber Regulations Advisory Committee and with the previous approval of the Central Government, by notification in the *Official Gazette,* make regulations consistent with this Act and the rules made thereunder to carry out the purposes of this Act.

2) In particular, and without prejudice to the generality of the foregoing power, such regulations may provide for all or any of the following matters, namely:

a) the particulars relating to maintenance of database containing the disclosure record of every Certifying Authority under clause (m) of section 18;

b) the conditions and restrictions subject to which the Controller may recognise any foreign Certifying Authority under sub-section (1) of section 19;

c) the terms and conditions subject to which a licence may be granted under clause (c) of sub-section (3) of section 21;

d) other standards to be observed by a Certifying Authority under clause (d) of section 30;

e) the manner in which the Certifying Authority shall disclose the matters specified in sub-section (1) of section 34;

f) the particulars of statement which shall accompany an application under sub-section (3) of section 35;

g) the manner in which the subscriber shall communi-cate the compromise of private key to the certifying Authority under sub-section (2) of section 42.

3) Every regulation made under this Act shall be laid, as soon as may be after it is made, before each House of Parliament, while it is in session, for a total period of thirty days which may be comprised in one session or in two or more successive sessions, and if, before the expiry of the session immediately following the session or the successive sessions aforesaid, both Houses agree in making any modification in the regulation or both Houses agree that the regulation should not be made, the regulation shall thereafter have effect only in such modified form or he of no effect, as the case may be; so, however, that any such modification or annulment shall be without prejudice to the validity of anything previously done under that regulation.

90. Power of state government to make rules

1) The State Government may, by notification in the Official Gazette, make rules to carry out the provisions of this Act.

2) In particular, and without prejudice to the generality of the foregoing power, such rules may provide for all or any of the following matters, namely:

   a) the electronic form in which filing, issue, grant receipt or payment shall be effected under sub-section (1) of section 6;

   b) for matters specified in sub-section (2) of section 6;

   c) any other matter which is required to be provided by rules by the State Government.

3) Every rule made by the State Government under this section shall be laid, as soon as may be after it is made, before each House of the State Legislature where it consists of two Houses, or where such Legislature consists of one House, before that House.

91. Amendment of Act 45 of 1860

The Indian Penal Code shall be amended in the manner specified in the First Schedule to this Act.

92. Amendment of Act 1 of 1872

The Indian Evidence Act, 1872 shall be amended in the manner specified in the Second Schedule to this Act.

93. Amendment of Act 18 of 1891

The Bankers' Books Evidence Act, 1891 shall be amended in the manner specified in the Third Schedule to this Act.

94. Amendment of Act 2 of 1834

The Reserve Bank of India Act, 1934 shall be amended in the manner specified in the Fourth Schedule to this Act.

THE FIRST SCHEDULE

(See section 91)

Amendments to the Indian Penal Code (45 of 1860)

After section 29, the following section shall be inserted, namely:

Electronic record

1. "29A. The words "electronic record" shall have the meaning assigned to them in clause (t) of sub-section (1) of section 2 of the Information Technology Act, 2000".
2. In section 167, for the words "such public servant, charged with the preparation or translation of any

document, frames or translates that document", the words "such public servant, charged with the preparation or translation of any document or electronic record, frames, prepares or translates that document or electronic record" shall be substituted.

3. In section 172, for the words "produce a document in a Court of Justice", the words "produce a document or an electronic record in a Court of Justice" shall be substituted.

4. In section 173, for the words "to produce a document in a Court of Justice", the words "to produce a document or electronic record in a Court of Justice" shall be substituted.

5. In section 175, for the word "document" at both the places where it occurs, the words "document or electronic record" shall be substituted.

6. In section 192, for the words "makes any false entry in any book or record, or makes any document containing a false statement", the words "makes any false entry in any book or record, or electronic record or makes any document or electronic record containing a false statement" shall be substituted.

7. In section 204, for the word "document" at both the places where it occurs, the words "document or electronic record" shall be substituted.

8. In section 463, for the words "Whoever makes any false documents or part of a document with intent to cause damage or injury", the words "Whoever makes any false documents or false electronic record or part of a document or electronic record, with intent to cause damage or injury" shall be substituted.

9. In section 464,

a) for the portion beginning with the words "A person is said to make a false document" and ending with the words "by reason of deception practised upon him, he does not know the contents of the document or the nature of the alteration", the following shall be substituted, namely:

"A person is said to make a false document or false electronic record:

"First, who dishonestly or fraudulently:

a) makes, signs, seals or executes a document or part of a document;
b) makes or transmits any electronic record or part of any electronic record;
c) affixes any digital signature on any electronic record;
d) makes any mark denoting the execution of a document or the authenticity of the digital signature, with the intention of causing it to be believed that such document or part of document, electronic record or digital signature was made, signed, sealed, executed, transmitted or affixed by or by the authority of a person by whom or by whose authority he knows that it was not made, signed, sealed, executed or affixed; or

"Second, who, without lawful authority, dishonestly or fraudulently, by cancellation or otherwise, alters a document or an electronic record in any material part thereof, after it has been made, executed or affixed with digital signature either by himself or by any other person, whether such person be living or dead at the time of such alteration; or

"Third, who dishonestly or fraudulently causes any person to sign, seal, execute or alter a document or an electronic record or to affix his digital signature on any electronic record knowing that such person by reason of unsoundness of mind or intoxication cannot, or that by reason of deception practised upon him, he does not know the contents of the document or electronic record or the nature of the alteration."

b) after explanation 2, the following Explanation shall be inserted at the end, namely:

Explanation 3: For the purposes of this section, the expression "affixing digital signature" shall have the meaning assigned to it in clause (d) of subsection (1) of section 2 of the Information Technology Act, 2000.

10. In section 466,

a) for the words "Whoever forges a document", the words "Whoever forges a document or an electronic record" shall be substituted;

b) the following explanation shall be inserted at the end, namely:

Explanation: For the purposes of this section, "register" includes any list, data or record of any entries maintained in the electronic form as defined in clause (r) of sub-section (1) of section 2 of the Information Technology Act, 2000".

11. In section 468, for the words "document forged", the words "document or electronic record forged" shall be substituted.

12. In section 469, for the words "intending that the document forged", the words "intending that the

document or electronic record forged" shall be substituted.

13. In section 470, for the word "document" in both the places where it occurs, the words "document or electronic record" shall be substituted.
14. In section 471, for the word "document" wherever it occurs, the words "document or electronic record" shall be substituted.
15. In section 474, for the portion beginning with the words "Whoever has in his possession any document" and ending with the words "if the document is one of the description mentioned in section 466 of this Code", the following shall be substituted, namely:

    "Whoever has in his possession any document or electronic record, knowing the same to be forged and intending that the same shall fraudulently or dishonestly be used as a genuine, shall, if the document or electronic record is one of the description mentioned in section 466 of this Code".

16. In section 476, for the words "any document", the words "any document or electronic record" shall be substituted.
17. In section 477A, for the words "book, paper, writing" at both the places where they occur, the words "book, electronic record, paper, writing" shall be substituted.

The Second Schedule

(See section 92)

Amendments to the Indian Evidence Act, 1872 (1 of 1872)

1. In section 3,

    a) in the definition of "Evidence", for the words "all documents produced for the inspection of the

Court", the words "all documents including electronic records produced for the inspection of the Court" shall be substituted;

b) after the definition of "India", the following shall be inserted, namely: 'the expressions "Certifying Authority", "digital signature", "Digital Signature Certificate", "electronic form", "electronic records", "information", "secure electronic record", "secure digital signature" and "subscriber" shall have the meanings respectively assigned to them in the Information Technology Act, 2000.

2. In section 17, for the words "oral or documentary,", the words "oral or documentary or contained in electronic form" shall be substituted.

3. After section 22, the following section shall be inserted, namely:

   When oral admission as to contents of electronic records are relevant.

   "22A. Oral admissions as to the contents of electronic records are not relevant, unless the genuineness of the electronic record produced is in question".

4. In section 34, for the words "Entries in the books of account", the words "Entries in the books of account, including those maintained in an electronic form" shall be substituted.

5. In section 35, for the word "record", in both the places where it occurs, the words "record or an electronic record" shall be substituted.

6. For section 39, the following section shall be substituted, namely:

What evidence to be given when statement forms part of a conversation, document, electronic record, book or series of letters or papers.

"39. When any statement of which evidence is given forms part of a longer statement, or of a conversation or pan of an isolated document, or is contained in a document which forms part of a book, or is contained in part of electronic record or of a connected series of letters or papers, evidence shall be given of so much and no more of the statement, conversation, document, electronic record, book or series of letters or papers as the Court considers necessary in that particular case to the full understanding of the nature and effect of the statement, and of the circumstances under which it was made".

7. After section 47, the following section shall be inserted, namely:

Opinion as to digital signature where relevant

"47A. When the Court has 10 form an opinion as to the digital signature of any person, the opinion of the Certifying Authority which has issued the Digital Signature Certificate is a relevant fact".

8. In section 59, for the words "contents of documents" the words "contents of documents or electronic records" shall be substituted.

9. After section 65, the following sections shall be inserted, namely:

Special provisions as to evidence relating to electronic record

65A. The contents of electronic records may be proved in accordance with the provisions of section 65B.

Admissibility of electronic records

65B. (1) Notwithstanding anything contained in this Act, any information contained in an electronic record which is printed on a paper, stored, recorded or copied in optical or magnetic media produced by a computer (hereinafter referred to as the computer output) shall be deemed to be also a document, if the conditions mentioned in this section are satisfied in relation to the information and computer in question and shall be admissible in any proceedings, without further proof or production of the original, as evidence of any contents of the original or of any fact stated therein of which direct evidence would be admissible.

2) The conditions referred to in sub-section (1) in respect of a computer output shall be the following, namely:

a) the computer output containing the information was produced by the computer during the period over which the computer was used regularly to store or process information for the purposes of any activities regularly carried on over that period by the person having lawful control over the use of the computer;

b) during the said period, information of the kind contained in the electronic record or of the kind from which the information so contained is derived was regularly fed into the computer in the ordinary course of the said activities;

c) throughout the material part of the said period, the computer was operating properly or, if not, then in respect of any period in which it was not operating properly or was out of operation during that part of the period, was not such as to affect the electronic record or the accuracy of its contents; and

d) the information contained in the electronic record reproduces or is derived from such information fed into the computer in the ordinary course of the said activities.

3) Where over any period, the function of storing or processing information for the purposes of any activities regularly carried on over that period as mentioned in clause (a) of sub-section (2) was regularly performed by computers, whether:

a) by a combination of computers operating over that period; or

b) by different computers operating in succession over that period; or

c) by different combinations of computers operating in succession over that period; or

d) in any other manner involving the successive operation over that period, in whatever order, of one or more computers and one or more combinations of computers, all the computers used for that purpose during that period shall be treated for the purposes of this section as constituting a single computer; and references in this section to a computer shall be construed accordingly.

4) In any proceedings where it is desired to give a statement in evidence by virtue of this section, a certificate doing any of the following things, that is to say,

a) identifying the electronic record containing the statement and describing the manner in which it was produced;

b) giving such particulars of any device involved in the production of that electronic record as may be appropriate for the purpose of showing that the electronic record was produced by a computer;

c) dealing with any of the matters to which the conditions mentioned in sub-section (2) relate, and purporting to be signed by a person occupying a responsible official position in relation to the operation of the relevant device or the management of the relevant activities (whichever is appropriate) shall be evidence of any matter stated in the certificate; and for the purposes of this sub-section it shall be sufficient for a matter to be stated to the best of the knowledge and belief of the person stating it.

5) For the purposes of this section,

a) information shall be taken to be supplied to a computer if it is supplied thereto in any appropriate form and whether it is so supplied directly or (with or without human intervention) by means of any appropriate equipment;

b) whether in the course of activities carried on by any official, information is supplied with a view to its being stored or processed for the purposes of those activities by a computer operated otherwise than in the course of those activities, that information, if duly supplied to that computer, shall be taken to be supplied to it in the course of those activities;

c) a computer output shall be taken to have been produced by a computer whether it was produced by it directly or (with or without human intervention) by means of any appropriate equipment.

Explanation: For the purposes of this section any reference to information being derived from other information shall be a reference to its being derived therefrom by calculation, comparison or any other process.

10. After section 67, the following section shall be inserted, namely:

Proof as to digital signature

"67A. Except in the case of a secure digital signature, if the digital signature of any subscriber is alleged to have been affixed to an electronic record the fact that such digital signature is the digital signature of the subscriber must be proved."

11. After section 73, the following section shall be inserted, namely:

Proof as to verification of digital signature

73A. In order to ascertain whether a digital signature is that of the person by whom it purports to have been affixed, the Court may direct

a) that person or the Controller or the Certifying Authority to produce the Digital Signature Certificate;

b) any other person to apply the public key listed in the Digital Signature Certificate and verify the digital signature purported to have been affixed by that person.

Explanation: For the purposes of this section, "Controller" means the Controller appointed under sub-section (1) of section 17 of the Information Technology Act, 2000'.

12. Presumption as to Gazettes in electronic forms

After section 81, the following section shall be inserted, namely:

"81 A. The Court shall presume the genuineness of every electronic record purporting to be the *Official Gazette*, or purporting to be electronic record directed by any law to be kept by any person, if such electronic record is kept substantially in the form required by law and is produced from proper custody".

13. Presumption as to electronic agreements.

After section 85, the following sections shall be inserted, namely:

"85A. The Court shall presume that every electronic record purporting to be an agreement containing the digital signatures of the parties was so concluded by affixing the digital signature of the parties".

Presumption as to electronic records and digital signatures

85B. (1) In any proceedings involving a secure electronic record, the Court shall presume unless contrary is proved, that the secure electronic record has not been altered since the specific point of time to which the secure status relates.

2) In any proceedings, involving secure digital signature, the Court shall presume unless the contrary is proved that:

a) the secure digital signature is affixed by subscriber with the intention of signing or approving the electronic record;

b) except in the case of a secure electronic record or a secure digital signature, nothing in this section shall create any presumption relating to authenticity and integrity of the electronic record or any digital signature.

Presumption as to digital signature certificates

"85C.The Court shall presume, unless contrary is proved, that the information listed in a Digital Signature Certificate is correct, except for information specified as subscriber information which has not been verified, if the certificate was accepted by the subscriber".

14. Presumption as to electronic messages

After section 88, the following section shall be inserted, namely:

88A. The Court may presume that an electronic message forwarded by the originator through an electronic mail server to the addressee to whom the message purports to be addressed corresponds with the message as fed into his computer for transmission; but the Court shall not make any presumption as to the person by whom such message was sent.

Explanation: For the purposes of this section, the expressions "addressee" and "originator" shall have the same meanings respectively assigned to them in clauses (b) and (za) of sub-section (1) of section 2 of the Information Technology Act, 2000.

15. Presumption as to electronic records five years old.

After section 90, the following section shall be inserted, namely:

90A. Where any electronic record, purporting or proved to be five years old, is produced from any custody which the Court in the particular case considers proper, the Court may presume that the digital signature which purports to be the digital signature of any particular person was so affixed by him or any person authorised by him in this behalf.

Explanation: Electronic records are said to be in proper custody if they are in the place in which, and under the care of the person with whom, they naturally be; but no custody is improper if it is proved to have had a legitimate origin, or the circumstances of the particular case are such as to render such an origin probable.

This Explanation applies also to section 81A".

16. For section 131, the following section shall be substituted, namely:

Production of documents or electronic records which another person, having possession, could refuse to produce.

"131. No one shall be compelled to produce documents in his possession or electronic records under his control, which any other person would be entitled to refuse to produce if they were in his possession or control, unless such last-mentioned person consents to their production".

THE THIRD SCHEDULE
(See section 93)

Amendments to the Bankers' Books Evidence Act 1891 (18 of 1891)

1. In section 2:

a)for clause (3), the following clause shall be substituted, namely:

(3) "bankers' books" include ledgers, day-books, cash-books, account-books and all other

books used in the ordinary business of a bank whether kept in the written form or as printouts of data stored in a floppy, disc, tape or any other form of electromagnetic data storage device;

b) for clause (8), the following clause shall be substituted, namely: (8) "certified copy" means when the books of a bank:

a) are maintained in written form, a copy of any entry in such books together with a certificate written;:: the foot of such copy that it is a true copy of such entry, that such entry is contained in one of the ordinary books of the bank and was made in the usual and ordinary course of business and that such book is still in the custody of the bank, and where the copy was obtained by a mechanical or other process which in itself ensured the accuracy of the copy, a further certificate to that effect, but where the book from which such copy was prepared has been destroyed in the usual course of the bank's business after the date on which the copy had been so prepared, a further certificate to that effect, each such certificate being dated and subscribed by the principal accountant or manager of the bank with his name and official title; and

b) consist of printouts of data stored in a floppy, disc, tape or any other electromagnetic data storage device, a printout of such entry or a copy of such printout together with such statements certified in accordance with the provisions of section 2A.

After section 2, the following section shall be inserted, namely:

Conditions in the printout.

"2A. A printout of entry or a copy of printout referred to in sub-section (8) of section 2 shall be accompanied by the following, namely:

a) a certificate to the effect that it is a printout of such entry or a copy of such printout by the principal accountant or branch manager; and

b) a certificate by a person in-charge of computer system containing a brief description of the computer system and the particulars of:

A) the safeguards adopted by the system to ensure that data is entered or any other operation performed only by authorised persons;

B) the safeguards adopted to prevent and detect unauthorised change of data;

C) the safeguards available to retrieve data that is lost due to systemic failure or any other reasons;

D) the manner in which data is transferred from the system to removable media like floppies, discs, tapes or other electromagnetic data storage devices;

E) the mode of verification in order to ensure that data has been accurately transferred to such removable media;

F) the mode of identification of such data storage devices;

G) the arrangements for the storage and custody of such storage devices;

H) the safeguards to prevent and detect any tampering with the system; and

I) any other factor which will vouch for the integrity and accuracy of the system.

c) "a further certificate from the person in-charge of the computer system to the effect that to the best of his knowledge and belief, such computer system operated properly at the material time, he was provided with all the relevant data and the printout in question represents correctly, or is appropriately derived from, the relevant data."

THE FOURTH SCHEDULE

(See section 94)

Amendment to the Reserve Bank of India Act, 1934 (2 of 1934)

In the Reserve Bank of India Act, 1934, in section 58, in sub-section (2), after clause (p), the following clause shall be inserted, namely:

"(pp) the regulation of fund transfer through electronic means between the banks or between the banks and other financial institutions referred to in clause (c) of section 45-1, including the laying down of the conditions subject to which banks and other financial institutions shall participate in such fund transfers, the manner of such fund transfers and the rights and obligations of the participants in such fund transfers."

Bibliography

Barkley, J., (1999) "Role Based Access Control." URL: http://hissa.ncsl.nist.gov/rbac/proj/paper/node3.html, Accessed 9 Mar., : 1.

Barlow, J., (1990) "Crime and Puzzlement: Desperados of the DataSphere,".

Carter, D., Katz, A., (1999) "Computer Crime: An Emerging Challenge for Law Enforcemen."

"Computer Crime." URL: *http://www3.bc.sympatico.ca/gja/980630.htm,* Accessed 9 Mar., 1999: 1.

Carroll, John Millar., (1977) *Computer Security.* Los Angeles: Security World Publishing.

Clark, Franklin, and Ken Diliberto (1996). *Investigating Computer Crime.* Boca Raton: CRC Press.

Coggins, James, (1980) "Practical Introduction to Computer Crime". *Colloquium given 2 September 1980.* Los Alamos, N.M.: Los Alamos Scientific Laboratory..

Comer, Michael J., (1985) *Corporate Fraud.* 2d ed. London and New York: McGraw-Hill.

Data Time, et al. (1989) *Computer Crime in South Africa.* Johannesburg: Data Time.

Ernst & Whinney, (1987) "Computer Fraud: A Report Presented to the National Commission on Fraudulent Financial Reporting". N.p.: Ernst & Whinney. Microfiche.

Francis, Dorothy Brenner, (1987) *Computer Crime.* New York: Lodestar Books.

Hafner, Katie, and John Markoff, (1995) "Cyberpunk: Outlaws and Hackers on the Computer Frontier". *1st Touchstone ed.* New York: Simon & Schuster.

Hafner, K. & Markoff, J., (1995) *Cyberpunk: Outlaws and Hackers on the Computer Frontier*, New York: Simon and Schuster.

Hanson, Wayne, (1996). "Future Crime" URL: *http://www.govtech.net/1995/gt/mar/future.htm* . Accessed 9 Mar., 1999: 1.

Hoffman, L., et al., "Cryptography Policy and Technology Trends." URL: *http://ftp.eff.org/pub/Privacy/crypto-policy_doe_94.report*. 1 Dec 1993, revised 30 Jan, 1994.

Koops, B. "Crypto Law Survey." URL: *http://cwis.kub.nl/~frw/people/koops/lawsurvy.htm*. Accessed 9 Mar., 1999: 1.

Shimomuro, T. & Markoff, J., (1996) *Take-Down: The Pursuit and Capture of Kevin Mitnick*, New York: Hyperion.

Strothcamp, Dave. *Fraud and Computer Crime*. Internet. URL: *http://www.csuohio.edu/accounts/Strothcamp/TOPIC07/sld001.htm*. Accessed 23 Feb., 1999: 1.

Varon, Elana, "Bill Would Double Budget to Fight Internet Child Pornography." *CNN Interactive*. Internet. URL: *http://cnn.com/TECH/computing/9902/12/fightporn.idg/index.html* . Accessed 24 Feb., 1999: 1-2.

Index